Reminiscences of the South Carolina Confederate Cavalry

Reminiscences of the South Carolina Confederate Cavalry

Including "Some Reminiscences of a Confederate Soldier," by Edwin Calhoun, and "Reminiscences of the Sixties," by Charles Crosland

THE UNIVERSITY OF SOUTH CAROLINA PRESS

An AccessAble Book. Published in Cooperation with University Libraries, University of South Carolina

New material © 2009 University of South Carolina

Cloth edition of *Some Reminiscences of a Confederate Soldier* privately published, n.d.
Cloth edition of *Reminiscences of the Sixties* published by the State Company,
Columbia, South Carolina, 1910
Paperback edition published by the University of South Carolina Press,
Columbia, South Carolina 29208

www.sc.edu/uscpress

Manufactured in the United States of America

17 16 15 14 13 12 11 10 09 08 10 9 8 7 6 5 4 3 2 1

Library of Congress Cataloging-in-Publication data is available.

ISBN 978-1-57003-813-6 (pbk)

THE following personal account of the experiences of Edwin Calhoun, 6th South Carolina Cavalry, Confederate State Army, was told to his daughter Eunice P. Calhoun (Mrs. Thomas S. Sease of Spartanburg, S. C.) when she was a child. Her notes, written in a childish hand, form the basis for this account.

DR. FRANK CALHOUN, EDWIN CALHOUN and JOHN J.
CALHOUN, taken at a Confederate Reunion. The three cousins
served together during the War and were very close until their
deaths.

SOME REMINISCENCES
OF A
CONFEDERATE SOLDIER

EDWIN CALHOUN
COMPANY C
6TH SOUTH CAROLINA CAVALRY
CONFEDERATE STATES OF AMERICA

ON THE NIGHT of December 19, 1860, at the home of her father, Mr. Edward Tilman of Monterey, South Carolina, Sallie and I were married. We had a big old-fashioned country wedding with lots of good things to eat and plenty of punch to drink. Our bridesmaids were Jenner Calhoun (Uncle Frank's daughter), Ida Calhoun (my sister), Carrie Calhoun (Mrs. G. E. Heard, daughter of John A. Calhoun), Sallie Norwood (Mrs. E. B. Calhoun), Fannie Fitch (Mrs. Jones), Fannie Calhoun (Mrs. J. W. Marshall), and Sallie Perrin (Mrs. George White). Our groomsmen were Hiram Tilman (Sallie's brother), Arthur Wardlaw (Mr. Alfred Wardlaw's son), C. A. Alexander, Jimmy Black from Columbia, Gilbert Tennent, and Charles Prioleau from Charleston.

Fannie Fitch, who came up for the wedding from Charleston on the 19th, brought the news that the State had virtually seceded on that day, although the Ordinance was not signed until the 20th. It was during the following month that I volunteered for military service, and on April 15, 1861, I entered the army, with Captain P. H. Bradley as my first Company Commander. I had just reached my 22nd birthday at that time.

Soon after I joined Captain Bradley's Company, we were transferred by rail from Abbeville to Charleston. My memories of the trip are not pleasant. The people on the train were drinking and cursing, which disgusted me very much, and when we reached Charleston it was dark, with no one there to tell us what to do. At last someone came and sent us to Shutz and Plats, which was a German sporting ground. Other companies comprising our regiment, commanded by Colonel Bacon, met us there.

Quarters were assigned to our company in one large tent, something like a circus tent. This arrangement was anything but satisfactory and comfortable. Little rest could be had, as some of the men were drinking, some were playing cards, and a general hubbub was going on the whole night.

I found other elements of life in the camp similarly disagreeable. Our diet consisted of baker's bread, fat bacon, and black coffee. The days were spent principally in drilling. The camp ground was low and marshy, and afterwards proved to be very unhealthy. All these things combined thoroughly disgusted me with soldier life, and I at once applied and received a discharge. Little did I think at the time that I was experiencing the pleasant part of soldier life.

Soon after I left the company, sickness in the regiment caused it to be moved to a location near Aiken. There they only remained a short time, as they were soon ordered into Virginia to take part in the First Battle of Manassas. I would have gone on with the regiment if I had not suffered a spell of bilious fever just at that time. I sufficiently recovered sometime in August and rejoined my company at Flint Hill, near Fairfax Court House in Virginia. Our life there was very monotonous as we had only camp and picket duty to perform.

We were ordered from there to Munson Hill, nearer the Potomac. From this place we could easily see the dome of the Capitol. Nothing of interest occurred here except an occasional skirmish with the enemy. A large cornfield lay between the two armies, and daily fights went on for possession of that corn. Sometime in November we were moved back to Cub Run, near Centerville, and ordered to prepare our winter quarters. Upon arrival there we occupied a temporary camp which was about a half mile from the place we expected to build our winter quarters.

The day after our arrival Lieutenants Cothran and Rogers and I went to Centerville, and during our return trip to camp we discovered in the road a large dead hog, which someone had shot. We concluded that the hog had been stolen by some soldier who was frightened away by our approach and since our rations were scarce at the time, we decided to appropriate the hog. It required the efforts of all three of us to drag the hog, which would have weighed 250 pounds net, about one hundred yards from the road into the woods. There we placed him by a log and covered him with leaves and brush. It was dark by this time and we intended to get our company wagon and haul him in that night so that the next day our mess and friends might have a

[6]

big feast. But imagine our surprise when upon our arrival at camp Colonel Bacon sent for Lieutenant Rogers and told him he had been reported for stealing a hog. Cothran and I escaped since Rogers was the only one the reporters knew, and he refused to tell on us. Colonel Bacon sent Rogers out that night to haul the hog into camp. He did not return until about twelve o'clock and brought no hog, since he could not locate the place we had hidden it. He was sent again the next day, but could not find it. A few days later we were clearing our winter camping ground when to our surprise we found the hog. This hog was one of twelve which Colonel Bacon had bought for the regiment from an old farmer nearby. A detail had been designated to kill these hogs as they could find them in the woods.

Shortly after this we moved into our winter quarters. Nothing of interest occurred at this camp, and we lived on the fat of the land. Just before Christmas our company sent a man up into the mountains to get chickens, turkeys, sausages and everything which accompanies a country hog-killing. He also found butter, sauerkraut, eggs, and plenty of Apple Jack. A merry Christmas we had.

It was at this camp that Major Seibles and Captain Bland fought a duel. Seibles was wounded in the breast, but soon recovered.

I mention here some of the officers in command, beginning with our regiment. The captains of the different companies were: S. J. Hester, White, B. Tolbert, Ham Brooks (a brother of Press Brooks), Holmes, Hardin, Sud Rogers, and P. H. Bradley. I was in Bradley's company. In our company, Wade E. Cothran was 1st Lieutenant, J. F. Calhoun was 2nd Lieutenant, and Theo. Rogers was 3rd. Colonel Tom Bacon commanded our regiment and Robert Fair was Lieutenant Colonel. Fair later became a Presbyterian minister after the war. Dr. Hearst was 1st Orderly. Emmet Seibles was Major, D. Wyatt Aiken was Adjutant; and old Charley Gray was drummer. The colonels who commanded the four regiments of the Brigade were: Bacon, Cash, Williams, and J. B. Kershaw. M. L. Bonham was our Brigadier General. Kemper's Battery was also attached to our brigade. General Beauregard commanded the forces in and around Centerville.

We remained at this camp until about the first of February, then we moved to the south side of Bull Run and camped in an old field. Since we were nearly a mile from any timber and since we had no wagons to haul with, all the wood we got had to be carried on our backs, and it was green pine wood at that. We were cold all the time —night and day—the snow was about one foot deep, and I have never

[7]

felt such wind in my life. It was terrible. Sometime in March we retreated to Rapidan and camped a few miles from Orange Court House. Here we joined General Earley's command.

A large number of hogs had been driven to this camp from the mountains and were being killed and shipped to Richmond. It was here that I saw one man open **six** hogs in one minute. Great numbers went every day to the slaughter pen to witness this.

About this time, General McClellan was preparing to advance on Richmond up the peninsular and was collecting his forces near Yorktown. This was about the last of March or first of April, and in order to meet this force, Earley's command was ordered to Yorktown. General McGruder was in command at this time at Yorktown. We were sent down the river from Richmond in boats to Yorktown, where we landed under heavy fire from the Yankees' gunboats.

Dams were built across a small stream which extended across the peninsular. This was done to prevent the Yankees from crossing, and a strong guard was kept at these places day and night. Soldier life began in earnest from this time on. We had heavy picket duty and constant skirmishing with the enemy by day and night. Our supply of clothing was scarce and rations still more so.

The bulk of the army had enlisted for twelve months, and our term of service expired on the 15th of April, 1861. So a few weeks after we arrived at Yorktown, General J. E. Johnston, who had taken command, called upon all the twelve month troops to re-enlist for one month. I think about nine-tenths of the men responded to the call and before the month was out the conscript act was passed by Congress which required military service of all men from twenty-one to thirty-five years of age. This included me as I was twenty-two. Soon after this, General Johnston began his retreat to Richmond.

At Williamsburg, Johnston made a stand in order to give his wagon-train time to get out of the way. General McLaw's division, of which we were a part, did the heaviest fighting. This was the first heavy fight we had been in, but our loss was moderately light.

And our command took part in McLaw's division's covering action during Johnston's long and tedious retreat from Yorktown to Richmond. Constant marching and countermarching, and fighting by day and night, was what we did until we reached the Chickahominy. I think I heard the commands, "Close up men" and "Double quick" ten thousand times on that retreat. Our feet became sore and blistered, and many threw their shoes away, while others carried them on their guns. We did not have a change of clothing, nor did we have time to change even if we had had the clothing. So by the time we reached Richmond we were both dirty and covered with vermin. I had been suffering for three months with dysentery and was totally unfit for duty. I was sent to Manchester Hospital at Richmond and through the influence of Dr. Bissel was discharged from service. It was not my intention to remain out of the army; I only wished to change from infantry to cavalry. Soon after I left, battles around Richmond were fought.

I reached home early in July, 1862, after an absence of about eleven months. Kate, my baby child, was nine months old. This was the first time I had seen her and it was hard for me to realize that she was my child. (This child later became Mrs. Cheves Haskell.) Soon after I got home, my father, Edward Calhoun, died. He was a devoted father and a pure, high-toned gentleman. Soon after his death I went to Columbia, S. C., and joined Capt. P. W. Goodwin's Co. C of the 6th S. C. Cavalry, which was commanded by Colonel Hugh Aiken, and which included Lieutenant Colonel S. P. Miller, and Major T. B. Ferguson. As we were undrilled in this branch of the service, it was thought best to keep us in camp for instruction for about two months. During this time Sallie came to Columbia and stayed at Mr. Black's, which made it very pleasant for me. It was like being at home to have her and Kate so near.

About the last of September or first of October we were ordered to Adams Run, S. C., to guard the coast below Charleston. Here we remained until the first of May, 1864, or about 18 months. Of course we changed our camp often during this time.

After we were fairly well settled at Adams Run, many recruits came to us and our company roll showed about 140 names. The officers of our company were Goodwin, Captain; Kennedy, 1st Lieutenant; Bailey, 2nd Lieutenant; Cobb, 3rd Lieutenant, and Clowney, Orderly. Dr. F. H. Calhoun was surgeon of the regiment. My mess included: J. J. Calhoun, John F. Donnelly (son of old preacher Jimmy Donnelly), G. H. Shands, and Ed Wilson. "Mike," a servant of mine, was our cook. Charley Calhoun, a brother of Dr. F. R. Calhoun, was also a member of our company. I was truly fortunate to have such men for mess-mates; they were all thorough gentlemen, and all-round jolly good fellows. John J. Calhoun, and I slept together and Shands with Donnelly. We always called John J. Calhoun, "John J."; Shands, "G. D."; and Donnelly, "Dad"; so after this I will call them by those names.

We had no fighting to do during our stay on the coast, but picket duty was very heavy. We lived well generally. We had plenty of beef and bread, and could frequently get potatoes, chicken, and, in winter, oysters. But if at any time our supplies became low, I would send "Mike" home, and Sallie would send me a well-filled basket, and would always put in at least half a dozen bottles of good old peach brandy, which we enjoyed very much, especially "Dad."

Once I sent Mike home for a box and wrote for a bag of peas also. I was on picket when he returned to camp with the box. When I got back to camp, I found "Dad" sitting by our campfire with his head resting between his hands. I asked him if he were sick. The answer was "no." Then I asked whether the box had come. "Yes," he said, and after a pause, and without raising his head, he muttered, "The box ain't worth a damn, not a drop of brandy in it." In the box we found a large turkey, a large ham, sausage, ribs, butter, light bread, cake, the bag of peas, and many other things in abundance. About a week later to our great surprise and joy, we found that Sallie had put the brandy in the bag of peas. Old "Dad," after he had taken several drinks said: "Well, boys, I think she (Meaning Sallie) is the best woman in the world."

Our company was frequently on detached service, and at one time when we were detached from the regiment, our camp was at Jenkins Farm. We called it Camp Jenkins. "John J.," "Dad," and I were fortunate in getting a crib to sleep in there.

Things went on in this way until we got orders to go to Virginia, which I think was about the first of April, 1864. We were allowed ten days furlough to go home, and were to report at the end of that time to Columbia. The second day after I left camp, in my eagerness to get home, I rode 76 miles without getting out of my saddle. We all met in Columbia at the expiration of our furlough, and started upon our long and tedious march on horseback to Virginia. At Winnsboro the citizens gave us a nice dinner which we fully appreciated. It rained a great deal on this march and since we had no tents we were wet nearly all the time. And to add to the hardships of the march, rations were very scarce.

When we reached Danville, Virginia, news reached us of the death of several Abbeville men. Arthur Wardlaw had been killed and General McGowan and Colonel Cothran had been wounded.

We reached Richmond early in May. No general battle was fought until June 12th, but we were constantly engaged in skirmishes with the enemy. On Wednesday, June 8th, three days' rations were issued, and the next morning at daybreak the whole of Hampton's Cavalry was in motion. We didn't know where we were going or what was up, but we felt as if a battle were pending. On Friday night we reached Louisa Court House. We could see in the distance the burning of a large mill. This was done by the Yankees, and we knew now that we were near. We were ordered to dismount and sleep with bridle in hand. All were soon asleep except those on guard.

During the night Oscar Sheppard, our Sergeant Major, awakened me and told me he was just from General Hampton's headquarters. He said that General Hampton had been out all night reconnoitering and had just returned saying he would attack the Yankees at sunrise the next morning. He reported that Hampton's brigades were well up except FitzHugh Lee, who was nine miles away but who would be there by sunrise. He was to protect the right wing, his position being at a church. I mention this to show what an important part this will have in the next day's fight.

Early the next morning the bugle sounded for us to mount. Our brigade was marched into a body of woods and there we counted fours, which meant that every fourth man was to stay in the rear with the horses, the other three going into battle. We then advanced and soon struck the Yankees, while we were still in the woods. Fighting commenced in earnest. We fought until about eleven o'clock, losing a good many of our men, among whom was my particular friend Oscar Sheppard. When he came to me the night before and gave me the information about the battle, he also said he expected to be killed in the fight, and asked me to see that his horse got back to his father in South Carolina, since it was a pet horse in the family.

Just at this time we were driving the Yankees and everything looked favorable for victory. To our surprise, however, our command was withdrawn from line of battle, ordered to remount, and we were marched instead to the rear where General Hampton joined us. We now saw the object of this movement; the Yankees had gotten in at our rear and had captured the horses of two regiments, also our wagon-train. General Hampton ordered a charge, and led it in person. It was a desperate hand-to-hand fight, but was soon over. We recaptured everything which had been lost, and also a good many prisoners. Just as this charge was over, a Colonel of artillery rode up and told General Hampton that if he would give him a squadron of men he would capture several pieces of artillery from the Yankees. Our company was sent. We

[11]

proceeded about half a mile down the road and found the enemy with the artillery. We were ordered to make the charge. We soon found it was heavily supported by infantry, which made it impossible for us to take. Three charges were made. It was very apparent now that the enemy had us completely surrounded. FitzHugh Lee, instead of taking his position on our right, where he was ordered, was four miles off. It was at this point where Lee should have been that the enemy got in at our rear. Nothing was left for General Hampton to do but cut his way out, which he succeeded in doing late that afternoon, falling back on Travillion Station. We lost the battle and Fitz-Hugh Lee was to blame for the whole of it. He had had plenty of time to take his position; in fact he had sent Hampton word that he was in position.

This battle occurred on Saturday, June 11th. That evening we formed a line up and down the railroad track, counting off. It fell to my lot to take charge of the horses, but as "John J." was sick, I swapped places with him and went into battle. Nothing transpired that night. The next day about nine o'clock, I was detailed to go on the outposts and remain there for several hours. Soon after I was relieved, the enemy advanced and the battle commenced in earnest. The way the land lay, the Yankees had the advantage of us and got possession of the depot and house. This served as a barricade for them. Shots poured forth from the windows and from behind corners. Our artillery then fired the depot, and as the Yankees ran out we killed most of them. The house was occupied by two women, so General Hampton gave orders not to open fire on it.

The fight was furious from now on; they charged our line seven times, but were driven back with considerable loss. Men were falling around me, and about three o'clock Tom Bradley was killed. A bullet had struck my gun and made it unfit for use, so since Bradley was the nearest man, I took his. There were two kinds of guns used in our company — a long Enfield and a short Enfield. Mine was the first, and his the latter. Of course my cartridge was too long to fit his gun, so I just poured his into my cartridge box. I got along alright until I got down to my cartridges, which were mixed with his; and then I had to look down and see that I got out the right one. While in this position, looking into my cartridge box, a bullet struck me in the left temple. A man by the name of Bell was right by me and afterward told me the bullet was fired by a Yankee who had gotten up into a big tree in front of the house. Another reason I am sure my wound came from this man was that many of the men around me were shot in the head, the bullets ranging downward.

Of course I was unconscious for several hours. When I did regain consciousness and learned where I was shot, I hadn't much hopes of recovery. It was almost sunset now and the battle was still raging as hotly as ever. I decided to try to get further up the line, where I thought the firing would not be so heavy. I crawled several hundred yards but found the fighting just as furious. Since I was weak with the loss of blood, I decided to lie there and take it. Soon after this the Yankees retreated and we had none to fight.

About ten o'clock the ambulance came around to carry the wounded men off the field and to take them to the field hospital, which was located in an old barn. On the way to the hospital we passed the spot where the horses were being held. "John J." asked the driver who he had in there and the driver told him right away that I was among the number. "John J." came around and asked me about my wound. I told him it was pretty bad, but I didn't think he would get my horse. Some months before we had made an agreement that which ever one was killed the other would get his horse. Both of us had very fine horses.

"John J." got in the ambulance and went to the hospital with me. With John's assistance I was able to get into the barn. Dr. F. R. Calhoun was inside busily attending to wounded men. I called him and he came right over, carrying a tallow candle in his hand. He was very much shocked when he saw the wound in my head, and dropped the candle saying "My God." I lay in a stupor most of the night and when I waked the next morning, Frank had gone on with the regiment, and I was in the hands of strange doctors. During the night I asked Frank if he thought I would get well. The only reply I could get was, "I hope so." Well, the doctors put me on the table, chloroformed me, and examined my wound. The bullet went in my left temple and lodged in the roof of my mouth near the pallet. The end of the bullet could be seen sticking out. During the day on Monday, John, who was sitting by my bed, asked what I wanted done with "Mike," my servant, and my horse. The doctor hearing him and thinking I was unconscious said, "Poor fellow, I don't think he will have much use for either in this world." I then told John I wanted him to keep them in camp for me, and that I would be back in sixty days. The doctor said I had twenty chances in one hundred, but the determination to get well had a great deal to do with it.

[13]

GEN. T. L. ROSSER'S CHARGE ON GEN. CUSTER'S DIVISION AND CAPTURE OF WAGON-TRAIN IN THE
BATTLE OF TREVILLIAN STATION
—JULY 11th 1864—

Private Chas. B. Reuss   Capt. Hatcher   Major P. B. Winston   Gen. T. L. Rosser   Color Sgt. John Nash   Gen. Custer   Gen. R. A. Alger
C.S.A.   C.S.A.   C.S.A.   C.S.A.   U.S.A.   Seizing His Flag   U.S.A.
      Capt. McGuire   Col. E. V. White   Major Holmes Conrad   Shot by Conrad and Falling   U.S.A.   Col. Clarke
         C.S.A.   C.S.A.   C.S.A.   with the Flag   U.S.A.

On Wednesday morning all of the wounded men were taken to the depot to carry them to the hospitals, the severely wounded to Gordonville and the men in a better condition to Charlottesville. I was booked for Gordonville, but asked that I be sent to Charlottesville, since I had been a student at the University of Virginia, and had friends there. There were probably a thousand wounded men at this depot. Those going to Gordonville got off on Thursday, but there was no train to Charlottesville until Saturday. There I had to lie from Wednesday until the train came on Saturday, all the while getting weaker and suffering very much with my head. For the first time I gave up and told John I did not believe I would ever get well. I felt as if a stimulant — whiskey, brandy, or something — would do me good. An old man, a citizen of the place, hearing me, went off and soon returned with a bottle of peach brandy, which revived me very much. When I had gotten a drink, the old man corked up the bottle, and remarked that he kept it for just such cases. As he walked off, John said, "Old rascal, I need a drink of brandy almost as much as you do." Just after this a young lady came to me and asked if there were anything she could do for me. I told her I would be glad if she could get me some food, for I had had nothing to eat since I was wounded on Sunday. She left and returned soon with a nice waiter of ham, chicken, bread, and buttermilk.

At last the train came on Saturday afternoon and we were carried in. Its jolting made the trip very painful for me, and I was unable to walk. When we got to Charlottesville, I was placed upon a litter and carried to the hospital. The next morning, Sunday, Misses Cable and Davis, daughters of Professors Cable and Davis, and whom I had known when a student at the University, came by the hospital on their way to Church. They recognized me and offered to do anything they could for me. They went on to Church where they saw Miss Willie Jones, also one of my friends. When they told her I was at the hospital, she did not stay for service, but came right out to me. From that time until I was able to go home she fed, nursed, and waited on me. I was confined to my cot for about three weeks and at the end of about five weeks I obtained a furlough to come home.

When I got to Richmond, I learned that the road below Petersburg had been torn up by the Yankees. Our regiment, fortunately for me, was camped near Richmond, and I got my horse, since it had been sent into the city with many others to be shod. My horse and I came down on the train until I reached the break in the road; then I rode horseback for about forty miles. Here I sold my horse and took the train for home. This trip on horseback was very trying, and I suffered a good deal with my wound.

When I reached home, I met Mr. James Norwood, who told me I had a little stranger at home, but could not tell me whether it was a boy or a girl. Right here I will say that I did not know I was blind in my left eye until I started walking around in the hospital at Charlottesville.

I remained at home until sometime in October, when I went to Columbia to have the ball removed. Dr. Chisholm performed the operation. He did not wish to make a cavity in my mouth and tried to force the ball down my throat; but instead of going that way, it lodged in a cavity in my cheek. I returned home and after a time the ball worked back to the roof of my mouth. I went to Dr. Chisholm again, and this time he was forced to make the cavity in the roof of my mouth to get the ball out. The hole is there today.

When I was shot, the ball passed through the brim of my hat,° carrying a piece of wool with it. Unknown to me, or to the doctors, this piece of wool remained in my wound, irritating it and keeping it from healing. The only wonder is that I did not have blood poison. Sometime after the bullet had been removed, the wool worked to the hole and I pulled it out with my finger.

My furlough expired sometime in November and I returned to our regiment, which was stationed near Petersburg, Virginia. My wound was still discharging, so I was pronounced unfit for service, and returned home. I was not able to rejoin the army as we surrendered in April.

°The wool hat that my father, Edwin Calhoun, wore when wounded is in the Confederate Museum, 1201 East Clay Street, Richmond, Virginia.

MUSTER
COMPANY C

6TH SOUTH CAROLINA CAVALRY
CONFEDERATE STATES OF AMERICA

GOODWIN, J. W., Capt.
KENNEDY, R. W., 1st Lt.
COBB, R. S., 2nd Lt.
BAILEY, W. A., 3rd Lt.
POWER, E. F., 3rd (after Bailey)

CALHOUN, F. H., Asst. Surgeon
CLOWNEY, JOHN, 1st Sgt.
WILSON, J. M., Sgt.
ROSENBOROUGH, R. A., Corp.
SMITH, A. J., Corp.

ALBERT, J. C.
ANDERSON, JAMES
ANDERSON, N., JR.
ANDERSON, R., SR.
ANDERSON, S.
ANDERSON, WILLIAM
ATKINS, J. T.
BEARD, J. M.
BELL, –
BOULWARE, R. D.
BOULWARE, J. C.
BOOZER, JAMES G.
BOYD, ROBERT
BLACK, A. B.
BURNETT, H.
BRINKLEY, W. R.
BROOKS, S.
CALHOUN, CHARLES M.
CALHOUN, EDWIN
CALHOUN, J. J.
CHAPPELL, G. S.
CLOUD, D. L.
CAMPBELL, J. J.
COLEMAN, JAMES
COBB, CHARLES A.
CRAIG, JAMES
CRAWFORD, W. H.

CUNNINGHAM, JOHN
CRUMPTON, S. H.
DAVIS, L. A.
DOUGLASS, T. G., DR.
DONNELLY, J. F.
GADSDEN, J. H.
FANNING, J. H.
FORD, W. N.
HALL, –
HALL, –
HUGHEY, SAMUEL
HUTCHISON, HENRY
HACKETT, T. L.
HUGHEY, J. L.
GLADDEN, WILLIAM
JOHNSON, –
JORDAN, J. B.
KELLY, WILLIAM
KENNEDY, E. A.
KENNEDY, A. B.
LOMAX, WM. A.
McCANTS, S. F.
McWHARTON, J. H.
McQUATTERS, S. T.
McKELLER, J. R.
MAXWELL, H. B.
MAXWELL, THOMAS

MICKLE, R.
MOORE, AUGUSTUS
PARKER, CHARLES
ROGERS, P. H.
ROGERS, H. D.
ROGERS, H. B.
ROBERTSON, J. W.
ROBERTSON, J. H.
ROSENBOROUGH, SAMUEL
ROSS, R. J.
SHANDS, G. D.
SANDERS, JOHN
SEAL, JAMES
SHADERACK, W. S.
SMITH, THOMAS
SMITH, E. S.
STEWART, JOHN
STACKMON, J. H.
STEWART, JAMES
SCOTT. WILLIAM
TENNENT, "FLY"
TRAPP, L. H.
VINNING, W. C.
WELBORN, J. G.
WILLSON, E.
WHITAKER, E. L.
YOUNG, JACK

SARAH TILMAN CALHOUN   EDWIN CALHOUN

These photographs were taken during the wedding
trip of Edwin and Sarah Calhoun in December, 1860.

WEDDING FIFTY YEARS AGO
Before The Time of Nice Bridal Gifts, Ribbon
Girls, and Pretty Marches to Delightful Measures.

Account of Wedding Reproduced
from
Abbeville Press and Banner

Heavily Laden Tables Furnish to Guests the Best of Meats
and the Sweetest of Sweets — Blazing Pine, and Not
Electricity, Made the Yard and Lawn a Scene of Light —
Sperm Candles Light the Mansion — Heavy Rainfall Ex-
tinguishes the Out-Door Lights, and Departing Guests
Grope their Way in Darkness.

Married, December 19, 1860, by Rev. DeWitt Burkhead, pastor of
Rocky River congregation, Mr. Edwin Calhoun of Willington, son of
Mr. Edward Calhoun, and Miss Sarah Smarr Tilman, of Monterey,
daughter of Mr. Edward Tilman:

BRIDESMAIDS AND BRIDESMEN

MISS IDA CALHOUN of Willington	MR. ARTHUR WARDLAW of Charleston
MISS FANNY CALHOUN of Calhoun Mills	MR. HIRAM TILMAN of Memphis, Tenn.
MISS FANNY FITCH of Charleston	MR. JAMES G. BLACK of Columbia
MISS SALLIE PERRIN of Abbeville	MR. CHARLES PRIOLEAU of Charleston
MISS SALLIE NORWOOD of Abbeville	MR. GILBERT TENNENT of Willington
MISS CARRIE CALHOUN of Abbeville	MR. CHAS. ALEXANDER of Washington, Ga.

OTHER GUESTS

Mr. James M. Perrin and his wife Mrs. Kitty Tilman Perrin. Mr. Perrin was killed at Chancellorsville, May 3, 1863. Mrs. Perrin died in Abbeville Sept. 7th, 1890.

Mr. Edward Calhoun, father of the groom, died during the war.

Mr. John F. Calhoun, brother of the groom, died at Clemson a few years ago.

Miss Rosa Calhoun, sister of the groom, married Mr. Charles Alexander of Washington, Ga., is living in 1910.

Mr. and Mrs. Charles T. Haskell died years ago.

Miss Mary Perrin, daughter of Mr. T. C. Perrin, married Col. F. H. Harrison of Anderson, and died years ago.

Miss Eliza Calhoun died in Washington, D. C., 1910.

Mrs. Wm. H. McCaw died in Mississippi.

Mr. George Speer is among the few survivors of that pleasant occasion.

Mr. and Mrs. Wm. Speer are both dead.

Miss Sophia Haskell married Mr. Langdon Cheves of Charleston, still living.

Mr. Joseph C. Haskell lives in Charleston.

Mr. Ephraim Power of Monterey is dead.

Mr. Alfred Wardlaw and Mrs. Ivy Tilman Wardlaw, his wife, lived and died in Charleston.

Miss Eliza Livingston married Mr. John T. Lyon, and still lives in Abbeville.

Dr. Yarborough, Mrs. Yarborough, Edward Yarborough, Dr. William Taggart, Major George Graves, Mr. Graves and Miss Mary Graves, all of Abbeville County are dead.

Miss Julia McCaw died fifteen years ago.

During the evening when the lovers were pledging their troth each to the other, said:

"I love thee, I love but thee
With a love that shall not die
Till the sun grows cold
And the stars are old
And the leaves of the judgment "book unfold."

WHAT BECAME OF THE WAITERS

A recital at this time of the names of those who lent the grace of their presence at this interesting occasion may not be uninteresting to the survivors. For that reason all the names that could be recalled are herewith appended.

Miss Ida Calhoun, sister of the groom, married Mr. Charles A. Alexander of Washington, Ga., and died several years afterward.

Mr. Arthur Wardlaw was killed in the battle of the Wilderness May 5, 1864.

Miss Fanny Calhoun married Dr. Joseph W. W. Marshall of Abbeville, where she still lives.

Mr. Hiram Tilman never married. He died at the home of his sister, Mrs. Kitty Perrin in Abbeville, 1876.

Miss Fanny Fitch married Mr. Jones. She lives in Columbia.

Mr. James E. Black married in Columbia and moved to Fort Smith, Ark., where he died years ago.

Miss Sallie Perrin married Mr. George White of Abbeville, where both are living.

Mr. Charles Prioleau never married. He died soon after the war.

Miss Sallie Norwood married Mr. Edward B. Calhoun. They moved to Atlanta where she lives.

Mr. Gilbert married and still lives in Augusta, the only groomsman living.

Miss Carrie Calhoun married Mr. George Hurd of Elberton, and is living there now, 1910.

Mr. Charles A. Alexander died a few years ago in Washington, Ga.

THE LIGHTS

The lawn and yard in front of the house were brilliantly lighted by great flambeaus, which were built of rich pine, resting on platforms covered with sand, and which was supported some five feet above

[20]

ground. These lights were in great profusion and servants were in attendance whose duty it was to keep them brightly burning.

The house within was lighted by countless candles and the light of many a heart were reflected in the light of beautiful eyes that spoke for happy hearts.

As was customary in those days, the wedding supper was of the solid and substantial parts, while the liquids that bring us victorious over all the ills of life were not absent.

The dining tables were laden with the meats. and sweets, served in all the various styles. For instance: The menu consisted in part of baked ham, roast pig with a big apple in its mouth but which it did not eat, turkey and trimmings, and all the sauces that please the eye and tempt the appetite. In an adjoining compartment, set apart for that purpose, the gentlemen were served with the best of Scotch punch, while the ladies elsewhere, were luxuriating in aromatic coffee, steaming hot and strong.

Except for the passing thoughts of the events which are said to cast their shadows before, all were happy. Guests from Charleston brought news of the State Convention, with assurance that the Ordinance of Secession and its probable results and consequences were discussed by all. While a few may have feared fatal results to some of that assembly yet none could foretell, or even imagine the disastrous consequences that came to the country.

1860   1910

GOLDEN WEDDING

(Account of Golden Wedding anniversary
taken from Abbeville Press & Banner.)

THE SOCIAL EVENT OF THE WEEK

SOME PLEASANT INCIDENTS AND THRILLING EVENTS
IN MR. CALHOUN'S LIFE

December 19, 1860 — Happily married to the most loving and devoted wife in all the land.

April 15th, 1861 — Patriotism called him to enlist in the war for Southern Rights. He went to the Army as an infantryman in the company commanded by Capt. P. H. Bradley.

August, 1862 — Serving a little more than a year, without wound or accident, he returned to his home, to which a little baby had come in his absence.

September, 1862 — Joined the cavalry service in the 5th S. C. Cavalry. Was in all the fights in which the Regiment was engaged, the company being in command of Capt. P. W. Goodwin of Greenwood.

June 22, 1864 — In battle of Trevillian, received wound which maimed him for life.

IN A DEADLY FIGHT

As well as we can understand, a sharpshooter on the firing line of the Union side climbed a tree to the height of about thirty feet, so that he might use his gun more effectively. The Yankee line of battle was driven back, while this sharpshooter remained in his vantage ground, but perilous situation. As the Confederates advanced they were in easy reach of his rifle and for a time during the storm of battle the Confederates had not discovered him. It is not known how many men this daring Union soldier killed, but under the tree in which he was stationed were many empty shells.

And it is certain, from the angle of the rifle wounds, a number of Confederates were killed and wounded by this man. It is unquestioned that it was from his fire that Mr. Calhoun was wounded when about fifty yards from the tree. Among the comrades of Mr. Calhoun the killed were Thomas Bradley, son of Gen. P. H. Bradley. On the battlefield.

> "He lay like a warrior taking his rest
> With his martial cloak about him."

The deadly conflict went on in all its terrible fury. Many were wounded or killed. Among others, a man named Cunningham and a comrade from Whitners Company, whose name Mr. Calhoun does not remember, were killed there. The Yankee sharpshooters deadly work went on until a wounded man named Bell from Fairfield fell to the ground from pain of a wound "his back to earth, his face to heaven." While on the ground he discovered the sharpshooter, and Bell aimed his rifle at him as he sat on a limb and at its fire the Yankee threw his arms around the tree, and then slowly loosened his hold of the body of the tree, falling from limb to limb until he was on the ground dead. James Morris, father of Rev. Leslie Morris was wounded at the same time and was sent to the hospital with Mr. Calhoun where Morris died. Jack Young of Greenwood lost a leg at the same time. The Company went into the fight with 64 men and came out with only 34 men.

CHILDREN OF MR. CALHOUN

The children of Mr. and Mrs. Edwin Calhoun are named in the order of their birth:

Miss Kate Calhoun married Mr. L. C. Haskell. They live in Abbeville. Their children are:

Miss Ella W. Haskell, Master Edwin Calhoun Haskell, Master Langdon Cheves Haskell, Miss Sarah Calhoun Haskell, Master Allen Wardlaw Haskell, Miss Kate Calhoun Haskell, "Children's Children are the crown of old men; and the glory of children and their fathers."

Mr. John F. Calhoun lives in Atlanta.

Miss Frances M. Calhoun is in Stonewall Jackson Institute of Virginia at Abington, Va.

Mr. Edward T. Calhoun was clerk in the store of Capt. John G. Edwards at Abbeville, when he was taken sick of fever, and died September 21, 1886.

"There is no flock, however watched and tended
But one dead lamb is there!
There is no fireside howso'er defended,
But has one vacant chair."

Mr. Arthur W. Calhoun, merchant in Hendersonville, N. C. He married Miss Marie Thomson.

Miss Sallie T. Calhoun, teacher in Greenville, S. C.

Mr. Charles A. Calhoun married Miss Janie Wright. They live in Denmark, S. C. One daughter has come to their home.

Miss Eunice P. Calhoun is at home.

Miss Ivy Calhoun, their youngest child, is with her parents.

PRAYER

Rev. H. W. Pratt, pastor of the Presbyterian church was present. He made appeal to the throne of Grace in behalf of the honored and beloved hosts, who are members of his church, and for those assembled.

We return humble and hearty thanks unto thee, our Heavenly Father, as the giver of every good and perfect gift. We thank thee that thou gavest us life, and hast sustained our lives. Because thou art good, we are all gathered here tonight.

We thank thee for the marriage relation which thou hast ordained, which thou didst establish in Eden, and which our Lord didst sanctify and honor by his presence when on earth, and which relation he has told us is a type of that glorious relation one day to subsist between himself and the Church.

We thank thee for the joy of this occasion. While many marriage ties are broken by the grim Reaper ere many years are passed, we thank thee that thou hast singularly blessed and prolonged this union for fifty years; fifty years of happiness, fifty years of service for God and for man, fifty years of consecration of themselves and their children to Jesus Christ. We thank thee that through the perils of war thou has preserved thy servant, the head of this house. We thank thee that thou hast warded off disease, accident, dangers, seen and unseen. So, too, we thank thee that thou hast kept in life until this time his devoted helpmeet, God's very best earthly gift to man. And we thank thee that she is here at this time by thy goodness to bring cheer and gladness by her presence.

We thank thee for this Christian home, with the children and grandchildren with which thou has blessed it, and we thank thee that tonight, after all these years, we can all gather here and give thanks unto the Lord, for he is good.

So great have been thy blessings in the past that we can only pray that they may be continued in the future. May thy servant and his helpmeet be spared yet for many years, to bring gladness to friends and loved ones. We pray thee to crown their latter years with plenty and comfort and if the Lord tarries when thy plans for them are completed here, we pray thee to give them and all their children an abundant entrance into thy presence.

We thank thee Father, lord of heaven and earth, for this assembly of friends and kindred. Bless those who have come from great distances. Bless the loving friends and neighbors who join in giving humble and hearty thanks for the example of good lives whose union we celebrate, and for all the blessings which we enjoy. Departing, guard and protect each and all to their respective homes. Bless their lives and save us all in thy Kingdom. We ask in Christ's name. Amen.

GUESTS

Last Monday evening, December 19, 1910, a large company of good people responding to the invitation of Mr. and Mrs. Edwin Calhoun, assembled in their home to take part in the celebration of the fiftieth anniversary of their marriage.

Among the friends and kindred who were out-of-town guests, we are furnished with the names of the following named ladies and gentlemen:

Mrs. Charles Alexander, Washington, Ga., sister of Mr. Edwin Calhoun.

Miss Carlotta Alexander, Washington, Ga.

Mr. and Mrs. C. A. Calhoun, Denmark, S. C.

Mr. J. F. Calhoun, Atlanta, Ga.

Miss Ida Calhoun, Clemson College.

Dr. Richard Calhoun, Augusta, Ga.

Mr. E. Calhoun Haskell, Greenville, S. C.

Mr. John Gass, Greenville, S. C.

Mr. J. J. Calhoun, Cartersville, Ga.

Mr. Lewis Wardlaw, Hester, S. C.

Mr. George C. Graves, Latimer, S. C.

Mr. C. G. McAllister, Latimer, S. C.

Miss McAllister, Latimer, S. C.

Mr. Hugh Middleton, Augusta, Ga.

Mrs. Sallie Gower, Greenville, S. C.

Miss Kitty Perrin, Greenville, S. C.

Mrs. Thedore DuBose Bratton, of Jackson, Miss., was Miss Ivy Perrin of this city. She married Rev. John Gass. After his death she married Bishop Bratton, whose wife she is today.

James Sumter Perrin, is an attorney at law in the city of Yazoo, Miss. He was born on the day that the first gun in the war was fired — at Fort Sumter — April 12, 1861.

Mr. George Smith of Calhouns Falls, S. C.

Mr. George Speer of Monterey was one of the few who witnessed the marriage of Mr. and Mrs. Calhoun fifty years ago.

Mr. Calhoun DeBruhl, Greenville, S. C.

Mr. Calhoun A. Mays, Edgefield, S. C.

All rooms and halls of the whole house were thrown open and every foot of standing room was occupied by the great assemblage of loving friends and kindred.

COMMITTEES

On Invitation To Dining Room

Mrs. T. D. Bratton   Miss Mamie Lou Smith

Mr. and Mrs. T. G. White

On Service In Dining Room

Mrs. C. A. Alexander   Miss Irene Rosenberg

Miss Carlotta Alexander   Miss Mary Taggart

Miss Ida Calhoun   Miss Helen White

Miss Kate Marshall   Miss Sallie White

On Distribution Of Souvenirs

Miss Sarah C. Haskell   Miss Louise McDill

On Hall Reception

Mr. and Mrs. C. D. Brown   Mr. and Mrs. J. H. McDill

On Sitting Room Reception

Mr. and Mrs. James Chalmers   Mr. and Mrs. W. S. Cothran

Miss Kitty T. Perrin

On Parlor Reception

Mr. and Mrs. Edwin Calhoun   And all the children of

Mr. J. J. Calhoun   Mr. and Mrs. Edwin Calhoun

Mrs. George White

AFTER FIFTY YEARS

In the golden glow of the evening tide of life, Mr. and Mrs. Calhoun opened the doors of their beautiful home on Greenville Street, to surviving friends of fifty years ago as well as to those friends of the younger generation, who have come into their lives.

The house was beautifully decorated in evergreen and yellow. Guests were ushered into the parlor where Mr. and Mrs. Calhoun received under trellises of evergreen suspended from the ceiling. In the center of the room a large wedding bell of white and yellow was suspended, touched here an there with sprigs of ivy.

From here guests moved to the dining room where a delightful course of salads and sweets was served.

On the centre of the dining table another bell of white and yellow was suspended and from it spengeria was gracefully looped to the four corners of the tables.

In the sitting room were tables spread with gifts beautiful in design and workmanship; such gifts as betoken the great love and esteem in which Mr. and Mrs. Calhoun are held.

The decoration of holly, mistletoe and ivy, with the color scheme of yellow and white made a beautiful setting for the lovely women and handsome men who moved hither and thither as pleasure directed. A prettier reception or a more pleasant occasion one could scarcely imagine.

Fifty years husband and wife! How few may follow this road to the goal! How few scarcely reach the summer of their years!

Looking back over their lives, Mr. and Mrs. Calhoun recall those who have fallen here and there by the way. On an occasion the memory of these comes up vividly in the minds of the bride and groom of fifty years. Hand in hand they have walked together along lifes way "bearing each others burdens, sharing each others joys." With their children and grandchildren about them, full of years of ripened experience, chastened by the hand of time, they may look with assured hope into the great beyond, as they recall with pleasure the past.

There is love in the warmth of youth; there is love in the practical life of the busy man and woman; but love in its fullness is found only in the feeble heart that still responds to that of its mate; when the form is bent and the hair is white with years.

The presence of Mrs. Fannie Marshall, the oldest of the bridesmaids and a most devoted friend of the family, was missed amid all the scenes of pleasure and happiness. She was unable, on account of the weather, to be present.

SQUIRE TILMAN

SQUIRE TILMAN

Squire Tilman was born in slavery on the Tilman plantation at Monterey, South Carolina. When the slaves were freed, "Uncle Squire," then a young man, chose to remain with his beloved "Marse Ed" Calhoun. As old age beset "Uncle Squire," father presented him with a house and a one horse farm and all the wood he could use as long as he lived.

When he grew too old to do the heavy work his sons did it for him. At the end of the year his sons told him that it took all the money the cotton brought to pay expenses. He came to father in great distress and asked him to take the farm back and rent it and give him the money. Father did this, and arranged with a merchant to let him have so much a month. "Uncle Squire" came to Abbeville the first of every month for his allowance. On one of these occasions, I had his picture taken. When I gave him one I asked him if he knew who it was. A broad grin came on his face. He said "Dats me. If I hadn't knowd it was me, I would have knowd it was my stick."

REMINISCENCES
OF THE SIXTIES

BY

CHARLES CROSLAND

BENNETTSVILLE, S. C.

THE STATE COMPANY
COLUMBIA, S. C.

PREFACE

As I have elsewhere stated, when I first wrote out these reminiscences nothing was further from my thoughts than publishing them. That was an afterthought. My family and family connections hearing of my writings asked to read them, they told their friends and family about it, and my little book passed into so many hands and was so generally commended that they, one and all, urged me to have it published. I at first treated it as a joke, but the solicitation became so general that I began to think seriously about it culminating into action. This is my apology for seeming to become an author and daring to write a book. I ask the charity of all.

CHAS. CROSLAND.

INTRODUCTION
1910

Having for a long time intended to write some recollections of my service in the War between the States—of course in the Confederate Army—thinking after I am dead and gone it would be a pleasant and useful legacy to my children, I now try to proceed to that task, being admonished that I am growing old and may at any time be prevented by the Great Reaper. I am especially aroused too to this task by the revival of war memories and scenes by the organization of our old veterans in Camp Hennegan and the reunion of same at Richmond, Va., to lay the cornerstone of the monument to our grand old leader Jefferson Davis.

I do not assume to write a book, but to record personal reminiscences, and am fully sensible of the greatness of my undertaking and my shortcomings and the imperfections of my work, on account of the lapse of time dulling my memory, and the trying times I have passed through since, politically and financially, and my want of scholarship. Nevertheless, I dedicate these pages to my children and their posterity.

CHAS. CROSLAND.

REMINISCENCES of THE SIXTIES

(COMMENCED JULY 14, 1896.)

Y first enlisting in the Confederate Army was in Capt. J. A. Peterkin's Company, Maj. A. D. Sparks' Battalion of Cavalry, at Mount Pleasant, near Charleston, S. C. Later on when this command was disbanded I volunteered in and joined Company H, Hampton Legion, mounted infantry. My captain was Jack Palmer, of Orangeburg; first lieutenant, A. M. Snyder, now of Kingstree, S. C.

The last year or more of the war I was detailed for special duty and taken from active duty in my company and sent to Gen. Mart W. Gary's headquarters to act as courier and especially to act as clerk to Lieutenant R. W. Boyd, of Darlington, S. C., and courier, who was on the staff of General Gary and was his ordnance officer. In times of battle I had to keep the ordnance train of wagons near the front and supplied with ammunition, during battle to keep in touch with Lieutenant Boyd and General Gary and keep the wagon train where they ordered it, and after battle to collect rifles and ammunition captured, assort the different kinds of arms and deliver them to the government laboratory in Richmond, Va.

My oldest brother, W. D. Crosland, volunteered from Wofford College into the Holcombe Legion, Captain Walche's company; was captured on a scouting raid and put in Point Lookout prison until near the end of the war. His regiment was fused into our brigade, the Seventh S. C. Cavalry.

When South Carolina Seceded.

When South Carolina seceded I was quite a boy and as my parents were very strict with me I did not have the run of the little town like many boys, but my father's patriotism on grand occasions when speechmaking was the order of the day got the best of him and I was allowed to venture out and hear the speeches. These speeches fired my young heart, and like other boys and men, too, I donned a red star cut from red patent-leather and attached to coat lappel with a small Palmetto button.

This soon gave place to a genuine Palmetto rosette which I wore with the pride of a grown citizen. In rapid order followed the secession of other States, then the capture of Fort Sumter by the Federals and its recapture by South Carolina troops, then the call for volunteers for the war. My father was a strong secessionist and came home every day from town and talked to the family about the war and its results, read us the papers, and no one can imagine the tumultuous feelings aroused in a boyish heart. I remember when calmer scenes gave place to these passionate interviews I would steal upstairs by myself and buckle my father's old militia sword around me and stick an old pepper-box six-chamber revolver in my. pocket and strut around the room with a martial air and imagine slaughter to the Yankees and glory to myself. I would have given five years of my life to have paraded around the plantation with these gewgaws in bombastic attire before the younger brothers and negroes. I would have felt like a hero, but my sensible mother, who never saw any success for our caurse from the first, though intensely Southern in sympathies, always nipped my folly in the bud. My mother, I must say in justice to her memory, was a native of Vermont, was highly educated and knew the temper of the Northern people and their vast resources, and believed the contest to be an unequal one and our failure inevitable at last. Wise woman.

Call for South Carolina Troops.

The next great event was the call for a company of soldiers for our county. One was raised at once of over a hundred men, many of them our immediate neighbors and friends and the flower of the country. They were soon armed and uniformed and daily drills and target firing on the public square was the big excitement. Finally, when all was ready these soldiers were off to scenes of action, only in a few weeks to be followed by calls for other companies. My eldest brother, W. D. Crosland, was off at Wofford College and he, too, soon enlisted in a company at Spartanburg and went to the front, so our family was at once into it.

My father employed always a private tutor and allowed the better families to send to our school in a small academy standing under the oaks where A. J. Bristow now lives. Rev. A. J. Stafford of the Methodist ministry was our teacher at that time, and he volunteered in the first company raised as a private and was soon elected chaplain of the regiment, the Eighth South Carolina

Volunteers. The regiment was stationed at Florence, S. C., temporarily, and it became my duty for weeks to carry Mr. Stafford to Society Hill, our nearest depot, every Saturday morning so that he might preach to soldiers on Sunday, and I would meet him at the depot early Monday morning to bring him home to teach the remainder of the week. We had to cross the river on a tedious old ferry boat, as there was no bridge then. These trips lasted until the regiment was called into active service. This left us without a school. My heroic mother, with the care of household duties, four house servants to look after, and the weaving and spinning of cloth for the plantation negroes (some 100) as well as her social duties, undertook to teach four of us in the family. She was in poor health, but her devotion to duty and indomitable determination and energy conquered all obstacles and she taught us well and kept all other duties up. She soon saw the loose rein that the war spirit was giving me, a license hitherto not allowed and was detrimental to my best interest, so when any cause interrupted school she put me to carding cotton with the common old cotton cards and then spinning it into thread on the old spinning wheel. I had my task to perform. From this I learned to weave cloth, and the discipline was good for me. My father's health was beginning to fail, which added greatly to my poor mother's duties, but bravely did she bear all on before her. She was so ambitious for her children that no obstacle would stop her. She took the idea to heart that I must be accomplished, and with all on her hands and heart that would have broken down most strong and healthy women she started me to studying French. Though I never looked into a book before, she made such progress that I soon learned to read it well and speak it fairly. I remember that I read the novel "Corinne" as a pastime by myself.

Time wore on this way, when to add to all my parents' other troubles news came that my brother, who belonged to the Holcomb Legion, then in Virginia and afterward made into the Seventh South Carolina Cavalry and transferred to Gary's Brigade, had been captured in the peninsula while doing scout duty. All were much distressed, because his band of scouts had given the enemy much trouble for a long time by their daring and brave deeds. They had long threatened to kill them if ever captured. After a long time we got a letter from him from Point Lookout prison, where he was carried after a personal examination and

threat from Beast Butler. Here he languished and came finally
more dead than alive out of prison by exchange in February,
1865. The horrors and torture of this imprisonment told severely
on my mother, but she hoped and prayed for the best.

Conscript Act Passed.

The strain of war was calling for all able-bodied men, and
finally the conscript act was passed, which forced all parties of
18 years and over to go into the war. I was now nearing this
period and my parents looked forward to more trouble, for the
land was full of trouble, many dead and households in mourning,
and nursing wounded soldiers who were well enough to get home
to relieve the military hospitals. I remember I often helped
mother tear up old linen and bolts of cotton and sew and wind
bandages to send to the front, and can now see my poor mother
again as her eyes at times would fill with tears as her mind would
take hold of the thought that she might be performing this
service for one of her own children. All these trials made her and
father very solicitous about my approaching eligibility for
service. They were especially so about me because I had been
very delicate from early childhood. I came very near losing my
eyesight from constitutional weak eyes. Such was my trouble
that at three different times I learned to read and three times
forgot it all again, as I was banished from books and all light.
Once I remained one year in a dark room with blankets (dark
ones) hung over the windows and lived in darkness and per-
petual night. I remember now the anguish I endured with my
eyes. My sight was despaired of, but finally good nursing and
heroic treatment pulled me through. I recollect wearing a seaton
(a scale of silk punctured in skin to keep up inflammation) in
back of neck for about a year. Added to this I was very dys-
peptic and suffered from intense sick headache spells, and was a
wreck generally. My parents, though patriotic and willing to
give their children to the service, felt that my going forward
was a pure and speedy sacrifice of life to no purpose, and coming
after older brother's uncertain fate, for often months passed with
no tidings and all felt that he must be dead, made them loath to
give me up. But the question pressed upon us. I, fired with
patriotic ambition and tired of home restraints, was eager to go,
while parents reasoned with me. Father urged me to remain.
Being rich and influential he offered time and again to get me an

honorable medical and military exemption, but I objected. I think he did, too, for I remained at home without protest some four or five months after I was 18 years old, but I became so restive under the restraint that finally father gave up and I enlisted at once in a cavalry company raised a short time before by J. A. Peterkin, which was located then at Mount Pleasant, S. C. How my poor parents suffered no one can tell now, as they never had any idea but that I would speedily return a corpse. My sainted and heroic mother at once fitted me out with a warm suit of home-woven woolen gray jeans, overcoat of same, a pair of plantation-made boots—for clothing and shoes from the stores were long since things of the past. The Confederate cavalry had to furnish their own horses, so father gave me choice of all his stables, and as we all had our saddle horses for pleasure I took one I claimed, a fine home-bred sorrel. Thoughtless and fool that I was, I went around and with light heart bade my boy and girl friends good-bye, and while my poor parents' hearts were breaking I was in great glee, and now even am ashamed at the additional sorrow I must have given them by my seeming indifference at the gravity of the situation. Just here I wish to say father gave me a nice little pocketbook which I carried through the war and it is now in my desk as a memento, also the backs of a once nice portfolio that I got in my Christmas stocking a year before. This I carried through the war and all my letters were written upon it. In said pocketbook is the last bill of money paid me for services as a soldier, also transportation ticket from Richmond home issued under governmental control and certificates from Doctor Baer of my physical condition and orders of transfer from my company to General Gary's headquarters of our brigade to act as a courier. These are mementos worth preserving.

On the Way to the Front.

On the 24th of December, 1863, mounted upon my horse with my clothes packed in father's medical saddlebags he used to practice with in his pioneer horseback professional career, after an affectionate adieu to the loved ones, feeling like a hero, I set out to join T. L. Crosland, who had joined same command and under whose fostering care father wished me to be launched into the wide world, for this was my first trip alone from home. T. L. Crosland then lived on the Peterkin place, now owned by the Alfords, near Maj. Z. A. Drake's and Dr. Lane's. I spent the night of the 24th at his house. That night a good snow fell, but we set out early in the morning of Christmas day, the first I had ever spent from home. We rode until dinner and after feeding and eating a lunch at Mrs. Murchisons, J. D. and William's mother, we rode on and spent the night at Marion C. H. Pushed on next day through snow and spent the night on the Great Pee Dee River banks at John J. Stubbs's, a former resident of our county. He was glad to see us and hear from his Marlboro friends. I was getting very tired now with such long rides and felt I was not such a hero at last. Oh, the frivolity of youth! Next day we crossed the Pee Dee at long ferriage as it was called. A large flat was rowed in deep water by four men and polled along, and in shallower places by iron hooks on polls hooking trees and bushes. It was four miles across and I got pretty scared. Applied that night for lodging at a very rich rice planter's house, but was refused. We asked as soldiers to be allowed to stable our horses and we would sleep with them in the straw, but were turned away. I rebelled and proposed to stay anyhow, but my Cousin Tom would not agree. Though very tired we rode on some four miles and stopped at a poor woman's house, only two rooms. Her husband was in the war. She took us in and said she had very little to eat but would divide with us. Gave us meat and bread and poor coffee and we laid on the floor before the fire and rested. In the morning the good woman gave us a bite and would take no pay from travellers or soldiers. We left her with God's benedictions. We contrasted her treatment with that shown us by the rich rice planter whose property we were to defend. We keenly felt the indignity. God will reward the poor woman, as she gave us "the cup of cold water in His name."

A long ride and crossing Black River by a rope ferry (afterwards Santee River by ferry four and one-half miles long ferriage, as all the water courses were very full) brought us almost in sight of Georgetown, where we spent the night with a poor man who did all he could for us but would take no pay. After crossing Santee we pushed on to McClellanville next day and were entertained two days by Marlboro men who were camped there doing picket duty, as the Yankee gunboats were hovering around. Lieut. Pet Drake, brother of J. N. and J. A. Drake, was very kind to us.

In Camp at Mt. Pleasant.

Next day, after a long and sandy ride, we arrived at Mount Pleasant, where our company was camped. We were gladly received and assigned quarters and arms and uniforms. Next day we went out on drill, battalion cavalry drill, Capt. A. D. Sparks, major commanding. I was green, but soon caught on, and fell into camp life as naturally as if I had been cut out for it. After drill was over we would run horse races on a large level field where we held battalion drill. Sometimes 30 or 40 horses would run at a time. So much for fun, but when it came to duty such as patroling the beach on Sullivan's Island on lookout for Yankee gunboats, or rowboats filled with soldiers, the fun disappeared. We would have to ride a mile up and down the water's edge three or four hours at a time until relieved, the wind blowing off the cold waves as it only can blow on the seashore. I would get so cold I would almost fall from my horse, then I began to wish I was at home. I have often seen a level spot on the sand by morning be blown into little hills. The only fire we could have when off duty was behind sand banks and made from boards torn from magnificent dwellings abandoned because under fire of the enemy's guns. Many of these houses were riddled with shot and shell.

While camped at Mount Pleasant the old Irish women's horses would be turned loose to forage on us, and all sorts of tricks were tried upon them to rid us of their eating our horses' feed. One night a lot of our boys tied an old camp kettle to one of these horse's tail hard and fast and filled the kettle with brickbats and turned him loose with a whip start. The old horse ran like mad all over the town, arousing every dog to barking and following—and there seemed to be a thousand; citizens turned out to see and join in the yell. Thousands of soldiers camped around caught on and yelled. It raised such a commotion that the Yankees, hearing the noise, concluded some demonstration was on hand. They threw up calcium lights from gunboats and land batteries, lighting up the islands so we could read print, and then began to shell every point. The roar was grand. General Ripley, in command, turned out all troops and appeared on hand with staff to know the cause, but no one would tell, and after midnight all got quiet again. So much for soldiers' pranks. They were like boys away from home and order and restraints. Many of them were men.

Courier Duty on Long Island.

After some weeks had passed with this sort of life, volunteers were called to go over on Long Island to do courier duty, and a love of adventure caused me to volunteer with five or six others. We crossed in a large flat rowed with oars from north end of Sullivan's Island, where a large fort and battery was located called Battery Marshall, over the inlet to Long Island. The tide was running out very strong and our men in charge of the flat came near losing control of it, and we came near being carried out to sea where a large gunboat was ready to pick us up. It was a life and death struggle. The waves were running high, we got so far out, and I was frightened in an inch of my life, but finally we got on *terra firma* safely. Our duty here was to go up on the far end of the island some ten miles and simply be ready to carry an alarm signal to Battery Marshall for a detail of infantry pickets there in case the enemy tried to land there or Bull's bay or Dewes' inlet, all of which were right at us. The gunboats were riding at anchor just off the beach all the time. We rendezvoued down a steep bluff covered with thick oaks and palmetto trees and slept, ate and did our cooking and warming here out of sight of the enemy. We had a comfortable place and were protected against the wind, but it was very lonesome away from all companions and the busy scenes about camp. We had an easy and lazy time here for a month. When off duty we would be quartered on the south end of the island in the only house on it and under the guns of Battery Marshall. Here we had a jolly time. The house belonged to a Mr. Sweeny, who ran an oyster farm. We would take his flat and large grabbs ten feet long and go out on the back inlet on low tide and grapple up boat loads of large single oysters to our hearts' content. We caught sheepshead fish, coons and opossums, as they could be killed with a stick they were so numerous. I went over to camp one day in a row boat after our mail, and on being delayed getting back at the appointed hour I was left. I was in a peck of trouble and feared discipline for being out of place. I tried to get several boatmen to row me over, but all said they could not without orders. One man told me to go and ask Captain Warley, captain of a battery near Marshall, to help me, and he would do so as he was a kind-hearted man. I was a timid and unsophisticated boy, but under compulsion I went to his headquarters, made my request and stated my difficulty. He was very kind, saw my youth and timidity and asked me who I was. When I told him, he asked if I was Doctor Crosland's son. I told him I was. He then became more kind than ever, said he knew my father well, would take pleasure in helping me then or any other time I needed it and to call upon him; gave me an order to some boatmen to row me over at once. I left him with many thanks and will always feel kindly to his memory.

Yankee Gunboat Blown Up.

One night while on duty on the upper end of the island we heard a most terrific explosion and knew some unusual event had occurred and in the morning we went out on the beach and found it was the Yankee gunboat Housatonic that had been blown up by one of our daring torpedo boats. The whole upper deck of said gunboat that day floated out onto the beach. A detail of hands were sent from Sullivan's Island and they cut away hundreds of dollars' worth of the rigging, brass and copper and her bell and sent all over to Charleston. I sent home a flat strip of the painted deck, with name and date, in a letter as a memento. We were relieved soon after this and went back to camp, and it felt like going home, a soldier gets so attached to camp and its surroundings.

Soon after this Charleston was stripped of every command possible, the troops being sent to Florida to the campaign there, and to cover our destination our company was ordered up the coast to Ten Mile Church, Porchers and other points to make a feint to draw attention of the enemy to prevent his sparing any troops. We went out every night on the beach and sent up military skyrockets of all colors to mystify the enemy. This was fun and there were many amusing incidents connected with it. There were alarms of the enemy landing several times, and as it was always late in the night there was much bustle getting out to the point. I remember one night some of us slept in Porcher's abandoned house piaza, and some of the boys sewed up each other's pants legs, and in the hurry to get under arms they had to carry their pants in their hands, and it was quite a joke. All the harm I saw we did was to scare some low-country negroes so badly by our demonstrations that they took boats and went out to the Yankee fleet. We soon went back to camp again.

Yankees Attempt to Capture "The Little Ida."

Soon after this a Yankee gunboat ran into the town of McClellanville, some thirty miles above us, after a blockade runner, and we were ordered up there (two companies and a battery of artillery). We got up there on short notice, burning for a fight. The rowboats full of marines from the gunboat had rowed with muffled oars up to the blockade steamer, captured her and got up steam and had started out to sea when, on being hailed by one of our sentries she refused to heave to, our battery put a shot or two through her deck, when she stopped. Our boats all were aroused and full of soldiers and made for the steamer. The marines were falling out of her and taking to their rowboats to get back to their gunboat some distance down the stream, but we caught the most if not all of them, put the steamer back to port again, and sent the Yankees prisoners under guard to Charleston. This was the first live Yankee enemy I ever saw, and they created quite an excitement in camp and aroused our martial spirit highly. We felt as large as if we had taken a city. It was quite an event in our quiet coast life. The steamer's name was "The Little Ida." She lay there, having put her cargo ashore, some time and after all got quiet left, and I heard got captured.

A Great Outrage.

We remained here several weeks looking for a renewed expedition from the gunboats, and then were put on duty by details going up some ten miles to the mouth of Santee River to look out for passing of gunboats up the Santee. We were put on picket up in the third story of an immense rice mill owned by a Mr. Blake, an Englishman. From there we could plainly see any passing into the broad mouth of the Santee. This was the largest and richest plantation I ever saw, the canals were ten feet wide and deep and had the finest fish in them. The soil was a foot or more deep and cornstalks grew as large as a man's wrist or ankle, as thick in drill as cane almost, and was as blue as indigo it was so rich. The owner had gone back to England, the plantation abandoned, slaves all gone, and everything looked as lonesome and dreary as death. There were over an hundred negro houses, two rooms and piazza, on long streets fronting each other, and under large live oaks. I have always wanted to see this place under cultivation and visit it again. Soon after this we were ordered to Mount Pleasant again, and then occurred an event that shaped my life differently and has ever been felt as then, one of the greatest outrages perpetrated on free men.

Hampton's Legion Recruited.

Hampton's Legion had returned from Tennessee very much cut up and decimated and was to be recruited, and Col. M. W. Gary was promoted to brigadier general if he could make a full regiment and mount his men. By some State manoeuvering and military conniving it was ordered that our company and Captain Vennings' of our battalion of cavalry should be disbanded as organizations and merged into the Hampton Legion, giving our men choice of giving up our horses to *old* Legion men, enlisting where we pleased, and twenty days' furlough, or go to Hampton Legion retaining our horses. Our officers got an inkling of this at McClellanville and our captain, instead of telling his men and letting them quietly go home and re-enlist elsewhere, kept it quiet and carried us into camp at Mt. Pleasant as though nothing unusual was on tapis. That night our camp was suddenly surrounded by a company of Confederate soldiers with fixed bayonets and loaded guns, our horses put under guard, and we were informed of the status of affairs. We felt greatly humiliated at this action. We having been accepted as soldiers by the government and had done honorable and hard duty for months, and then to be treated this way was more than we could bear. Some of us tried to cut our horses' throats before we would give them up, but on going to them were not allowed access. Then we intended to foot it home, but we found ourselves fixed and shut up to the two courses above. We were in a tumult, all mad, some determining to do one thing and others another. While we were in this state we assembled in the piazza of a large house we were quartered in, and held an indignation meeting. We felt Capt. J. A. Peterkin had betrayed and deserted us, and I, among others, gave him our opinion and said very hard words to him, hard to take. I was especially insulting, but he took it all quietly. Since and after the war we have talked it over often and laughed over it. Many gave up their horses and joined bomb-proof commands, and got exempted and in one way or another evaded any further active duty. It was a great mistake for the service, for had we been put in Hampton Legion, or any other command, as an organized body we *all* would have gone with alacrity and been a power united, but as it was hardly a third went into the Legion or active service anywhere else. Captain Peterkin got a bomb-proof and was never any more good. I afterwards learned the whole truth about the transaction. He was under compulsion to hold us together till we could be transferred into other commands, and had he not done so would have been hardly handled.

From here on till the close of the war I enlisted and belonged to Company H, Hampton Legion, Gen. M. W. Gary's Brigade. I, among others, including T. L. Crosland, Edwin Coxe, D. C. and P. M. and J. T. John, Travis Pate, C. S. McCall (our orderly sergeant), Robert Stanford, William and Robert and Arthur Calder, P. M. Hamer, Alex Heustiss, Joshua and J. K. Fletcher, and others whom I do not recall now, all concluded on due consideration that we wanted to see active service and did not wish to be forced to give up our horses, so joined Hampton's Legion and went to Virginia. It took some hours to settle all this and write our transfers and furloughs, which done, some went home at once, others, along with a detail from the Legion, took charge of our horses and carried them up to Columbia, where the regiment was stationed. I sent my horse along by my negro boy father gave me for a cook and waitingman and I with T. T. Crosland and others took train for home. We landed at midnight at Society Hill, could get no conveyance home and set out on foot for same; got to the river and could not get old Doub, the ferryman, up to put us over. We shot his house and shouted all to no purpose and laid down on the river bank and slept until daylight when the old coon got up and put us over. We then set out afoot for home. There was a great rejoicing then. I came home a hero instead of dead or half so. I was so fleshy my parents hardly knew me. I had been fed on delicacies all my life, hardly ever sat down to dinner with less than three courses, and then suddenly transferred to active outdoor exercise of the rigid sort, eating the plainest food and less quantities I lost my dyspepsia and fattened like a pig. I remember Miss Constantia Townsend, one of my chums, sent me a large sponge cake in a box mother made up for me, and when I got it I sliced it, fried it in bacon grease with my meat and ate it with greed and thought it the best cake I ever saw. It greatly amused Miss Constantia and the homefolks when they heard how the cake was served. Our rations on coast were a little bacon, meal and sometimes flour, changed by rice and blue beef, mostly the latter, and it was tough eating as there was not an eye of grease on the beef and the rice was glue.

The Battle of St. Mary's Church.

We were to have all met at Columbia after ten days' furlough was out and gone to Virginia in a body, but about five days at home found me with a well-developed case of measles, and I was in bed very sick when my furlough was out. Father sent on a doctor's certificate, backed by statement of enrolling officer, and got my time extended. As I had a bad time it was three weeks before I was well enough to go forward, and then left sooner than my parents thought prudent as my extension was out and I feared consequences. On about the 28th of May, 1864, I started equipped again for Virginia via Columbia, S. C. Of course all were loath to see me go again, as now I was to be where there was great carnage and all felt very doubtful if I ever returned. I got to Columbia and found camp, of course, broke and all in Virginia, my boy riding my horse through the country with the regiment. I went direct to Richmond via Danville, and as cars were crowded rode with other soldiers on top the coaches to Richmond from Weldon. My eyes were nearly out when I got there, but as soon as there I was conveyed at once to the soldiers' home at the old Exchange Hotel and there I cleaned up and spent the night, and in the morning started out with others to the front in search of my regiment. I came up with it about June 25th, just after the battle of Cold Harbor was over, found it near Chickahominy River, at Ridley's Shop, near the enemy, in rifle shot, and went on duty at once, our horses being in rear in charge of every fourth man as was usual when we went into action. We lay under cover here a week or more speaking in low voices and whispers, looking for battle every hour. We could not cook or raise the least smoke. All the rations we had was cornbread baked some ten miles in rear and sent us in corn sacks thrown over backs of mules, and raw bacon. When the bread reached us it was mostly sour and broken into small fragments and crumbs. It was hard fare but all we could get, the raw meat was a pill with sour bread, but necessity knew no law and when we were hungry we ate it with relish and learned to love raw meat, and afterward often ate it so from choice when we had all chances to cook it. We organized our Marlboro friends into a mess at once, consisting of T. L. Crosland, P. M. Hamer, D. C. and P. M. and J. T. John, Edwin Coxe, Alex Heustiss, Travis Pate and myself. My negro boy and Coxe's boy did our cooking when we were in camp long enough to cook. We remained near Ridley's shop in small skirmishes and picket firing for several days. After an unusual hot fight all night and day with the enemy on this line we went into camp hungry and worn out, many of us too much so to wait for food, and fell down as soon as horses were unsaddled and fed, and went to sleep. About two o'clock in the morning a courier came up from St. Mary's or Samaria Church, some twenty miles, with orders for us to join Hampton. The bugle rang out for us to saddle up and fall in. I never was so much outdone, it seemed I had just gotten to sleep. We were in our saddle in ten minutes and on the road, and well do I remember that ride. The dust was ankle deep on the horses, and as we rode in two file the dust was so intense that we could not see the horses immediately in our front, nor could we see our hands held up before our faces. It came near suffocating us and I spit out great mouthfuls of pure mud. I thought I would die, and can't now see how I helped it, but a man can get used to anything, and nature became so overexhausted that I fell asleep finally in my saddle and rode on so for miles. Just about sunup we came to our destination, were ordered to graze our horses five minutes, and before we had more than dismounted and given them a bite we were ordered to mount and forward. We filed into a very large field and found many thousand cavalry there all drawn up and under a review by General Hampton. We were among the last to pass him, and as we did so with battle flags waving and bands playing and us hurrahing, the old general uncovered to us, his old regiment, and he told us he knew we would do our duty as of old. As each command passed him they were led out of the field and placed in position for battle. We were marched over a mile to the left and on counting fours were dismounted and with our long Enfield rifles went forward as we always did during an engagement. We crossed a large piece of woods which was fresh burned off to destroy the undergrowth to prevent the combatants from being concealed from each other and so take each other unawares. We passed through this woods driving a thin skirmish line in, under a scattering fire till we came to a rail fence around a field. Here we were halted and could plainly see the enemy in large numbers some half mile distant drawn up in line of battle.

They were soon charged by our men on our right flank—
Georgians and North Carolina troops. We could plainly see each
line of battle with their colors in front. Our line swooped down
upon them, both firing till they were very near each other, when
under a very hot and rapid fire from the enemy our men fell back.
Our men had muzzle-loading rifles and the Yankees had breach-
loading and rapid firing rifles and had so great advantage over
us. Our line reformed and went up on the enemy a little nearer
than before only to be repulsed again, but they fell back only a
short distance, reformed and charged the third time sweeping all
before them. It was a grand and inspiring sight. We knew the
enemy was only being driven under cover of his artillery and
expected to be called to support this charge each moment, and
sure enough we were ordered forward over the fence at double
quick. Word passed down the line that we were to charge a
battery, which always was dreaded by a soldier who knew what
it meant. Many a prayer went up, and aloud, too, but on we
went, and as we plunged into a piece of woods on the other side
of the clearing I ran right up on a large soldier badly wounded
and being carried out by four men. He was streaming blood and
groaning loudly. It completely unnerved me, as I said to myself
I am going where he came from. I would have run then at
once had it not been for my pride, but I pressed on, and we soon
fell upon the enemy in a swamp with the gaulberry bushes ten
feet high. We halted and fired at each other here at close range
till our guns got so hot we could scarcely hold them. We could
tell where the enemy were by watching the tops of the bushes
shaking. All of a sudden some one gave the alarm "fall back",
and we fell back a short distance. When the mistake was discovered we advanced again, driving the enemy before us. We
suddenly emerged from the swamp and got into an opening. Our
company ran up into a farmers' back lot and I ran into his horse
lot and saw the Yankees in full retreat, in fact stampeded. There
was a wide lane from this lot toward a field and it was jammed
full of a blue mass running for dear life, shedding guns, haver-
sacks and accoutrements as they went. I rested my rifle across a
cart in the lot and fired down this lane into the mass as fast as I
could load till they got out of sight. We then double-quicked
after them, and a mile further on, as expected, found they had
run under cover of their batteries. We were ordered to charge
these batteries planted on a high crown of hills. On we went

amid a storm of grape shot and cannisters and shells till we got
about a quarter of a mile of them, when Major Arnold, commanding our regiment, halted us, as we were out of ammunition, and
he said he would not sacrifice his men under such a fire. We laid
down under orders in a field of wheat just headed out, for protection, until we could get ammunition and support. I was completely broken down now, no food for 24 hours, and an all-night
march, and a battle with so much running, the heat intense, and
the excitement and yelling together with the intense burning pro-
duced by burning powder, caused a reaction as soon as I got quiet.
I was detailed then, with a squad from my company, to go to the
rear and bring back a turn of ammunition. We took the back
track and when about a half mile to rear we ran across a well of
water with about twenty-five soldiers around it almost fighting
for their turn to drink. When I came up I begged for water, and
moved by my size and youth and pitiful distress, I suppose, all
with one accord gave way to me, and said, "Give the boy water,
the poor little fellow needs it." I remember how thankful I was,
and they stood back and saw me drink. I thought I never would
get enough. The kind-hearted man who held the bucket warned
me I had better not drink too much as it would hurt me, asking
me if this was not my first battle, but inexperience and present
distress goaded me on, and I drank my fill and sat down to rest
a moment, and sure enough soon had cramp in my bowels and
could not move. I lay down in great agony and soon knew almost
nothing and thought I was dying. Kind passers tried to help me,
but could do nothing. I laid on the ground all that evening
until late in the night before I came around, then I was so weak
and worn-out I could not travel. Near me were three wounded
Yankees, one moaning all night, one just breathing, uttering no
sound, and the other died very soon. I fell asleep as soon as my
pains allowed, and when I awoke the sun was away up. I sprang
up and started to search for my command. I soon found it resting and about ready to go back to camp at Malvern Hill, where
we started from. This fight we called the battle of St. Mary's
Church—some called it Samaria Church.

In Camp at Malvern Hill.

Grant was crossing to the south side of James River, and his cavalry and some infantry were making this diversion to cover his movements. I omitted to mention that the first time in this battle that we felt the enemy in force was at the church, a neat white-painted building. The Yankees had felled the trees for breastworks, cut off the limbs and taken the benches from the church and pinned them to the logs, and they made it hot for us behind them, but we soon ran them out. We learned after the fight was over that the afore-named battery was captured and driven off, and our mounted cavalry drove the panic-stricken enemy we routed so into the river and many of them were drowned. When we got back to camp we were nearly famished and had an awful ride back through the dust. We went into camp at Malvern Hill, getting our water out of a huge spring at the foot of the hill, running from under a large gum tree; spout of spring was three feet across. We remained here several days doing picket duty along the river, where the Yankee gunboats lay in sight. The marine band discoursed beautiful music every night, which we enjoyed very much. We could hear them giving orders, too, and any common conversation. Under cover of trees and hills intervening we grazed our horses by order and in order each morning early and late in the afternoon in clover fields waist high bought by our quartermaster for the government. We had to avoid raising any dust to prevent being shelled by the enemy, which was often done. We lay here three or four weeks, having weekly and sometimes daily skirmishes with the marines from gunboats and Federal cavalry raiders who always were harassing our front.

Put to a Severe Test. Shoots a Yankee.

One day, hearing an unusual skirmish fire some mile or more distant, we were ordered out to the front, and found the fight to be one over the possession of some hogs our boys had shot near the river to supplement our short rations. The Federal pickets came forward to dispute possession, and a spirited fight occurred. The enemy landed more men to support pickets and our men supported ours, and the fight became general, involving all our brigade. We drove in their picket line and held the hogs, but they became then a small factor. Blood was up on both sides and the hog incident was forgotten. After driving in their skirmish line under cover of their guns or gunboats we were halted and formed into a close skirmish line up and down the river road, lined in our front with heavy oak forest with thick undergrowth of gaulberry bushes and other thick growth. We were posted behind every convenient large oak tree for protection, as the fire from the concentrated enemy was severe, and the gunboats, in addition, were shelling us, but we got so close under their guns it was hard for them to reach us, but they soon put mortar shells upon us, dropping them all around us. The infantry charged us several times, but were repulsed. They had a skirmish line much stronger than ours, and with superior breach-loading rifles and ours muzzle-loading, were vastly in advantage over us. However, we held our line under a very trying fire. Here I was put to a severe test and shot a Yankee, the only one I ever *knew* I hit. These were the circumstances: One interval of our line found no convenient tree for protection, so our captain (Jack Palmer) stationed a man some thirty yards forward of our line behind the trunk of a large whiteoak tree. The enemy were not slow in learning of his disadvantage and crossed fired him so sharply that they ran him from the tree, and another man had to be sent there at once to fill the gap, which was done. When in a few moments he was run in, a third and tried old Legion man was then sent there, but fire became so hot that he, too, soon retired. The enemy seemed to become generally aware of the situation and concentrated their fire upon this point and coming up nearer to it, as it was so much in advance of our line they could do so with comparative safety, under cover, too, of the undergrowth, and our rear was an open field. It looked like our line would be broken, when our orderly sergeant (Mat Dannerly) ordered me to go forward and hold the tree and post. I felt it unwarranted and told him I would not go, and demanded him to send back the men who belonged there. We were passing hot words when Captain Palmer came up and said, "Yes, Crosland, you are right; he cannot compel you to go, but it is important, and I ask you to go for my sake." Appealed to in this manner I could not refuse, and as all eyes were centered upon me and how I would bear myself, a new man, so to speak, among the old Legion men, I felt my opportunity to place myself upon the same plane with the old men (who felt themselves superior in valor) had arrived, and forward I sprang under the applause of new and old men. I expected to be killed before I reached the tree, but I got there safely and found it the center target of all that section of the line. The cross firing was so hot and accurate I was sure each moment was my last. I tried firing upon them, too, at first, but soon gave it up as I exposed my elbows loading my muzzle Enfield rifle. Their balls were ripping the bark off the tree all around, from the ground ten feet up, and cutting off twigs and leaves all around my head, as it was a very low-branched tree. I cannot now look back and see how I escaped except through a special Providence. My comrades to rear, right and left shouted words of encouragement to me as they loaded and shot at the advancing line of enemy. Among these especially was P. M. Hamer on my left and P. M. John on my right, both of my mess. All yelled to me to stand close up to the tree. I tried to do so, but the roots were large and high, projecting from the tree, and I could not stand close behind without leaning forward, and this was a very straining posture; however, I maintained it with much fatigue, under stern necessity, for an hour, the balls fairly raining upon the tree and around me and shells dropping and exploding just in my rear. It was very demoralizing, but pride held me to my post. It was now getting late in the afternoon and the enemy made a last rally and dash. I could hear their tramp just ahead of me, and hear them telling each other how to shoot to get me, hear all they said. Nature was about exhausted, standing in this position, and I had in this interval had all I ever did to pass in review before my mind. I was desperate and felt I had as well be killed one time as another and was about to change position and get a shot myself and risk consequences when their line became visible to our men. Philip M. Hamer called quickly and urgently for me to look out, that the enemy were upon me, and to fire. I sprang from behind the tree and not 20 steps from me I saw three bluecoats in a huddle with guns seemingly upon me, advancing through a thick clump of gaulberry bushes. As quick as lightning I fired upon them as by inspiration, feeling like the crucial time had come. I suppose the suddenness of my nervous fire took them by surprise. One of them fell yelling like a goat with his head hung in the fence. I sprang behind the tree, loading my rifle, looking each second to get the contents of the other two rifles at muzzle points. The suspense was awful, but short, for as the fellow fell yelling our whole line fell to cheering and applauding me. Comrades Hamer and John, especially exultant, calling to me that I had killed him, for all felt for me as I was such a small strippling sent to so trying a place. As soon as I got my gun loaded, which, you may be sure, was in an incredible short time, I sprang out again to die game, but instead the other two bluecoats had taken up the one I brought down and hustled him to the rear, and he was yelling at every step. I peered anxiously through every opening and watched the tops of every clump of bushes to detect any enemy passing through foot of same, but none came. This seemed to put a quietus on things, for in a few moments their line was withdrawn and we remained in line an hour longer, when our scouts reported all safe and quiet in front and we were ordered back into camp. This little episode fully established me in the confidence and esteem of the old men, and especially my officers. Captain Palmer was always very kind to me. This fight occurred very near an old jug manufactory called the "Old Pottery," and we soldiers called it the "Fight of the Old Pottery." What it is termed in history I do not know, and perhaps no mention is made of these smaller engagements except in reports of officers of the army to their superiors in rank.

Placed on Picket Duty and Forgotten.

Soon after this we moved camp and I was detailed, with four others, on the usual picket duty, and was sent to Long Bridge, over the Chickahominy River, to warn of the approach of the enemy in that direction. We carried our usual two days' rations with us, which, being scant, we ate up in one day, expecting to fast the second day, but we were not relieved as promised at the expiration of two days and our fast was prolonged. At the end of the third day I was nearly famished. We tried to buy or beg of a poor woman near by enough to stay our stomachs, but she was nearly as bad off as we were. She said Sheridan had been through there twice, and had succeeded in leaving starvation behind him as was his boast. We dared not abandon our post, yet were in a serious condition. I found a plum thicket of green plums and some worn-eaten ripe ones. I ate some these and wandered off and found some red green blackberries and tried these, then drew my cartridge box strap tight to draw my stomach up to fit the rations, drank water to fill up, and continued tightening my belt. I lived this way, taking my turn on duty three hours out of each twelve, until the end of four days, when a courier came to call us in, saying that our camp had been moved and a fight been on hand and we were overlooked. But we were rejoiced at relief, as now we were nearly starved, and after a ten-mile ride found our camp. When I got there our mess had on the fire a huge camp kettle of rice, bacon, beef and Irish potatoes, the latter stolen out of a good woman's garden by T. L. Crosland while P. M. Hamer talked to her at the front gate. This hash was soon done and I fell to on it and ate it hot from the fire and thought it the grandest meal I ever sat down to.

The Battle of Deep Bottom.

Soon after this, on the (dates have escaped me), we were hurried out of camp one morning, after being in a skirmish fight all day, having ridden twenty miles and gotten into camp past midnight, into the battle of Deep Bottom. When we reached camp above I was so tired out I unsaddled my horse, fed him and fell at his feet with my head on the saddle, without food, into a deep sleep. In the night a heavy rain came up, but I was so worn out that it never waked me, and when the bugle rang out to saddle up and the orderly came around arousing the men I got up out of a hole of water, half my body being submerged in it. I felt I had been asleep only five minutes, but threw my saddle on my horse and put my coat on, mounted, and was on my way to the front in less time than I can write. It was long before day. We rode some five miles, were dismounted and sent to the front. We threw out a skirmish line in front and forming in battle line in rear followed up the skirmishers until we got to the river road; here we came up with our skirmish line, who were feeling the enemy lively. In our rear was a heavy growth of oak timber, and in our front a large field of corn about seven feet high, just in the bunch to tassel. It was very thick and the enemy were there in large numbers. We lay in a little ditch about a foot and a half deep, its bank being thrown up and a low plank fence put upon it. We had not been here long when the enemy charged us, and we poured our fire into them, loading and firing as fast as we could. They came within fifty yards of us, then fell back, and in a short time formed and came again, this time getting within thirty yards of us. The fire from their gunboats and field artillery was fearful, the shells hissing, shrieking and bursting all around us, tearing off whole tree tops and limbs in our rear; the grape and cannister making a fearful rattling and sickening thud, striking tree trunks, was very demoralizing. They were so thick it sounded like a handful of wheat thrown among dry leaves in regard to multitude of sounds, and like lightning and hail striking many times a minute. We repulsed this charge handsomely, but only to be confronted with a line of battle three deep very soon after, with our's only one deep. This time they came within twenty steps of us and we could see the bluecoats well among the corn, now thinned by the fire. It looked like they would drive us out this time, they outnumbered us so much, but as fast as we fired we laid down in the ditch to reload, and up and fired again. I had fired my rifle so fast and often now that it became so hot I could hardly hold it in my hand. It got powder foul and as I tried to clean it a Yankee saw me and fired at me. The ball tore through the 12-inch plank at bottom of the fence and the spent ball hit me with a thud. I thought I was done for, but soon found I was o. k. The splinters of the plank hit D. C. John, who lay just beside me, in the back of the neck, and he thought his time had come, but finding his mistake we both got ready to fire about the same time, and putting our rifles through a crack of the fence we pulled upon the bluecoats. The fire getting rapid and no yelling going on, they supposed we were there in great numbers and were ready to mow them down when a little nearer, so they broke and ran. During this fire Captain Nickerson, afterward our major, was shot in the lower leg, and the pain was so intense that he yelled fearfully and jumped all over the road in our right, in an agony, holding his knee in both hands. It came near demoralizing our men. Just then the Twenty-fourth Virginia Cavalry, which belonged to our brigade and were posted to our right and held a ravine crossing the road, gave way, and the enemy, pressing on, outflanked our line. General Gary dashed up the road and ordered us to charge down the road and cut them off and retake the line, but the men on our right never moved, consequently we lay still. The general took out his pistols and threatened to shoot us if we did not move on. He ranted and fumed, but the men were dogged and remained firm, and we soon learned our right failed to move because they saw the utter futility of the action. They were largely outnumbered, and we were then nearly surrounded, and it was sure death to get up and move down the road under such a terrific fire. General Gary soon saw it, too, and ordered us to fall back a short distance, where he had ordered our led horses up. We mounted and at a brisk trot barely escaped from the cordon nearly around us. As we got beyond danger some one gave the alarm, "The

Yankees were upon us", when the order came "Gallop, march."
J. T. John's mare began to fall and stumbled twenty steps, when
she fell upon him, hurting him right badly. As we rode along I
saw a small piece of cornbread some one had dropped, and
though the regiment had ridden over it, I sprang down quick as
lightning and got it and went to eating it greedily, and thought
it the sweetest bread I ever ate. As we passed out of this battle
we passed Kershaw's brigade of infantry on our right, who had
been in the fight, and as they retired from the temporary works
the enemy crawled into them, and, strange to say, neither fired
upon the other, though immediately upon each other, in speaking
distance. This was a mystery to all of us. We lost a good sprink-
ling of men in this fight.

A Dangerous Picket Post.

Soon after this I was detailed to go on a very dangerous picket
post near Chafin's Farm, on the James River. We were carried
about four miles from camp in the night through a dark piece of
woods I had never been in before, and on a creek side in a deep
hollow the reserve post was established where the reliefs slept
while one was on duty. I was carried a mile further on, over a
long bridge, through a deep valley and up a long, high hill and
posted there on the edge of a large field of felled oak timber which
was as dry as tinder. Several hundred yards off lay a Yankee
gunboat where we could hear the bands playing and orders
given. I was warned that every night for a week we had lost a
man on this post from another regiment, and it was a post of great
danger. The sergeant instructed me if advanced upon to gradually fall back, and if suddenly, to fire and fall back when all
would come to me. He then left and went to reserve post. I was
very lonesome and scared. Every motion of my horse, creaking
of saddle and champing of bit sounded as loud as a gun to me. I
was straining my ears all the time to detect the least noise in my
front. After a time I heard a noise like a hog among the dry
bushes in front of me. It stopped often, then inched on, gradually
getting around me. I fell back twenty steps, when all was still
for a time, then it worked again the same way, and finally I lost
the noise. All of a sudden I heard it again nearly in my rear
flanking me. I at once fell back again. When after a time it
began again I was about to fire upon it when, greatly to my relief,
I was relieved and another comrade put on. I warned him and

went back to post. Away past midnight we heard a rifle shot and all hurried to the assistance. He reported the same facts I had given and fired upon it. We remained with him till day, when we were relieved by another squad from the regiment, and that night a man was taken off. It was the worst and most ticklish picket duty I ever did. I thought that night of all I ever did in my life, expecting death or capture. I could hear my own heart beating in the stillness of the night.

The Battle of Fuzzle's Mill.

Not long after this we got unexpectedly into the Battle of Fuzzle's Mill. We were quietly moving camp one day, our ambulances and wagon train with forage and cooking utensils and baggage being ahead, apprehending no danger, when our pickets ran in to us to give alarm of the advance of the enemy, but they were fleetly mounted and pressed hard on our pickets, riding into us simultaneously with our own pickets. The first thing we knew we were fired into, and our wagon and ambulance train made a summersault and ran back among us who were leisurely riding in their rear. We were completely taken by surprise, but General Gary rode up opportunely, as he always did, and ordered Major Arnold to dismount a squadron at once and hold the enemy in check until we could form the brigade and repulse them and get our led horses to the rear. He promptly did so, none too soon, for they came on thick and fired into us lively. It fell to my lot in counting fours to be No. 4, and I had to ride my horse and lead three others, taking care of all baggage, etc., feed and water them. I had always rather go into a fight than do this. I remember I offered to take T. L. Crosland's place, telling him he had a family and I had none, if either were killed, but he would not, and I led off my horses to the rear, leaving our boys in a stiff fight and not seeing them again for three or four days. Thus I cannot detail this fight, though near it and hearing often from it by guns and messengers.

Mr. William Murchison, an invalid, had just joined us here, being forced into the army, and was with the hospital crowd and came near being captured. The Yankees shot a volley at my negro boy and others at the same time, calling him to stop, but he ran like the wind and escaped. It was said he ran fifteen miles before he took up. He was the worst scared negro I ever saw. As he passed me I shouted to him to stop and ride one of my horses, but he needed no horse, one could not have caught him.

This fight was a series of sharp battle for several days, in which we suffered considerable loss. I was worried greatly with my horses, keeping them fed and watered and keeping the blankets under saddles, which was a job; with no rider they were always working out; then keeping luggage on saddles, running night and day hither and thither with them to be in reach of men if needed and out of reach of the enemy, who often stampeded us to capture them. I was rejoiced when I was able to see each man mount and take possession of his own horse. This was the battle of Fuzzle's Mill.

Assigned to Duty at Brigade Headquarters.

Soon after this I was ordered to report to brigade headquarters at once. I was at a loss to know what it meant and thought I had been reported for some action. Being a boy I could not imagine what was up. I arrived there and called at Lieut. R. W. Boyd's tent, to whom I was ordered to report. He received me kindly and asked me to write a sentence on some paper on his desk. I was puzzled and wrote one, boy-like, thus: "To spell well is a great merit, to spell imperfectly is a great demerit." He looked at it, smiled a little, and asked me if I had any idea what was wanted of me. I told him I did not. He then told me that Dr. H. Baer, my old school teacher, then in the surgeon general's office in Richmond, had gotten him, an old friend, to have me detailed from the regiment to remain with and to act as ordnance clerk and courier to him and Gen. M. W. Gary, he being on the latter's staff and brigade ordnance officer. I was much elated, as it meant higher duty, better rations and immunity from picket duty, though more danger in battle, as I must be always mounted and more conspicuous, and at the heels of General Gary all the time, who never feared danger and was always under fire. I went back to camp and got my little plunder and negro boy, bade my mess good-bye and took up new quarters at headquarters. The general had about eight other couriers, among them M. W. Tribble, of Anderson, Dan C. Tompkins, of Edgefield, a young Hamilton, of Laurens, Hughes, of Union, J. T. Sloan, now of Columbia, Albert Nickerson, of Edgefield. I soon fell in with these and became a favorite with them and was kindly treated by the general himself, and Lieut. R. W. Boyd treated me with the kindest consideration, for I was his ordnance clerk, too, and under his especial charge as he was ordnance officer of our brigade and of General Gary's staff.

Col. A. C. Haskell Wounded.

Soon after this we had quite an engagement at Malvern Hill and drove the enemy away with considerable loss. We were at this time in almost daily fights of minor importance and skirmishes as our brigade was set on the north of James river between Richmond and Pamunkey River for the local defense of the capital, while the main army of Lee was south of the James confronting Grant. Sheridan, Kautz and Wilson, of the Federal army, were always trying to turn our left flank and so capture Richmond, and several times came very near doing so. On one of these occasions Yankee troops were massed secretly in our front and a desperate charge made upon us, but we drove them back with loss, but the battle assuming much importance General Lee sent Longstreet's Corps across the pontoon bridges on the James River to our aid and finally came himself, and we had quite a desperate engagement. In our front were the Yankee cavalry and artillery in vast numbers. Our regiment and the Seventh South Carolina Cavalry were sent in to the charge, and the fight was so hot our men were pressed back by much superior numbers till finally Col. A. C. Haskell and General Gary dashed to the front and our color-bearer with them, when our flag fell into the enemy's hands. Here Colonel Haskell ran bluff upon Sheridan, Kautz and Wilson and in an instant hesitation which one to bring down with a fine pistol, a rifle ball from the enemy ploughed through his head and eye and brought him down. The enemy closed around him, took his watch and ring from him and at the same time our colors. Haskell was much loved by our whole brigade, and our men became infuriated and made a desperate dash upon the enemy, retook the body of Haskell, recaptured our flag and drove the enemy back with great slaughter. And here our company immortalized itself again, for at this juncture I came upon them riding out of battle to the rear after the engagement was over upon eleven pieces of fine artillery with horses and all (our men were mounted upon the horses) guns, caissons, caps off, hurrahing.

This was an inspiring scene, and just during this battle was the only time I saw General Lee closely. He had ridden up with his staff around him, and while he planned and surveyed the situation his minor officers lolled and rested on their horses. One younger officer, with some petulance, remarked louder than he meant that he was tired and sleepy and that he "had slept not a wink last night." General Lee calmly turned and simply remarked, he had slept scarcely a wink in a week. The young officer wilted.

Just about this time the fall of Ft. Harrison occurred. We were waked up one morning after fighting all day and getting to camp and sleep supperless about midnight, about an hour before day, by the bugle call to saddle up, were hurried to the front at a lively rate to New Market Heights to the rifle pits, then pushed to left to our earthworks, where the enemy, behind a mass of negro troops, were charging our thin line. We had hardly got to the breastworks before the enemy rushed en masse upon us and the works cheering tremendously. Here Will Simmons, of Charleston, one of our company orderlies, was killed, together with Sergeant Dannerly. Simmons jumped upon the works and swore he would have one good shot, when a rifle ball took him between the eyes and he fell backward dead. We lost a good many men here and were driven pellmell back. The great hoard of cavalry and infantry who had secretly been massed in our front, against only our one brigade, drove us wildly back before Lee could send us help from across the river. We had a running fight to the next set of earthworks, made a stand, but were as chaff before the wind. We ran in a panic for the line of works farther back commanded by Ft. Harrison. Here we made a desperate stand, but with only a few heavy artillerymen to aid us could do nothing against such numbers flushed with victory. We had to abandon the fort and whole line, and it looked now like nothing could save Richmond. We rode straight across the country, through creeks, mill ponds, with no regard to roads, pushing to our left all the time, for by this time Lee was pushing us help over the river from the right, and as fast it came we gave way further to the left. We ran into the inner line of breastworks and high forts in sight of the city barely in time to save them. General Gary with three or four of our couriers behind him, in advance of our line, found General Pemberton, of Vicksburg fame, in command, the latter calmly sitting his horse overlooking the scene. Our forts were bristling with heavy guns and artillerymen alone, and below in the valley some 1,000 yards away the enemy were massing for a final charge by the thousands. They could easily have ridden into the city, but evidently felt we had a large force and were preparing for them. It was dusk now and all the houses in our front, which

were many, had been fired to prevent the enemy's sharpshooters
from picking off our artillerymen. The heavens were lit up with
lurid lights, all was bustle and excitement, guns booming to our
right, the fight raging between Longstreet and the enemy all
along the line, and we calmly looking on, our foes ready to walk
in on us. Here General Gary rode passionately to the forts and
ordered the artillery to open on the advancing enemy. They
replied they were under orders from Pemberton not to fire. Gary
then rode up to him and after some remonstrance openly defied
him and charged him with intention to sell Richmond as he did
Vicksburg, and ordered the officers present to open fire. Pemberton at this rode to the rear, and seeing this the artillery,
already eager, opened every gun and the music began. It was the
grandest and most inspiring sight I ever witnessed. Sheets of
flame broke forth and shell, shot and grape were hurled into the
dense mass in our front. They stood it only a few moments, then
broke, panic-stricken at the carnage, and dashed for a mill dam
in their rear, over which they had poured just before. Our guns
were trained upon this, literally mowing a lane down along it
as they ran. This saved us, and in an hour's time our little crowd
was upon the mill dam, pushing on to the extreme left, where the
enemy was still pushing. The pond and both sides of the dam
were piled in heaps with dead men, horses, cannons, caissons,
blown up by our shells. The carnage was awful.

Stroicher, of Orangeburg, Avenged.

General Gary took his couriers steadily on to the left, sending
one hurrying up our brigade to' follow, and sent me with the
ordnance train through the city, then out ·upon the Nine Mile
Road to meet him and our troops there. Richmond as I passed
through was wild with excitement. Had the old men and boys
mounted on private and livery horses sending them out with such
arms as they could pick up. I found the Nine Mile Road blocked
with stampeded ambulance wagons, supply teams and city troops,
but pushed on with my wagons until I found General Gary. He
took us immediately to the front to our breastworks, and had
scarcely gotten there when we heard the thunder tramp in an
old field of pines of thousands of feet, and orders directing the
advance of the enemy. In a few moments they broke into sight.
Three lines of negro troops backed by a line of whites and white
officers. The negroes were drunk and bellowing and driven on

to the charge. On they came with few shots fired, our brigade hurrying as fast as possible forward, but the enemy were closer to the works than our men. We had a small field battery just to the left of the works enfilading the advance of the enemy, and they poured in their fire mowing down the men. We sat our horses impotently looking on, helpless, with balls whizzing by our heads. Just then our battery, seeing the enemy were upon us and in the works first, limbered up to leave, when Gary spurred his horse up to them, directing one more volley. As it was delivered the Yankees were pouring in a huddle up to and around it, and it made a sickening lane and havoc as it belched forth its last volley. Some of the riders cut their traces and escaped, others were captured, and then and there Sergeant Stroicher, of Orangeburg, was bayonetted, after surrender, by the enemy. We got off to the rear slowly and reformed our line some miles back about two hours after dark and started for the front again very quietly to recapture our lost works. We burst upon them suddenly and after a short and sharp fight drove them out, capturing some 400 or 500 negroes and a few white soldiers. They fled panic-stricken, throwing away their arms and baggage as they went. We worked the negroes and prisoners all night fearfully, strengthening our works, looking for a new attack in the morning, which never came.

In the morning General Gary ordered the prisoners carried "to Richmond," which meant kill them. They were told to cross the breatsworks and run, and they might go, when they were shot down like dogs in retaliation for the murder of Stroicher after surrender. I was sent out to gather up the abandoned arms and I took up eight wagon loads of them and carried them to the laboratory in Richmond. The field was dotted with dead negroes and white officers. The negroes had just been paid off and had plenty of greenbacks in their pockets and tintypes of their women at home. The ground was covered with codfish and hard tack. In assorting the different pattern of rifles I had the muzzle of one in my hand pulling it when it discharged, the ball passing through my coat sleeve, wristband and out at my back, going through side of my coat at body. It frightened me worse than the battle did.

Richmond's Narrow Escape from Capture.

Here ended the narrowest escape Richmond ever had of capture. Our cavalry followed in pursuit, driving the enemy pell mell into the Chickahomony swamp, when it was thought imprudent to go any further from our supports and we returned. This was the last grand attempt to capture Richmond from the north side, and aside from continual picket duty and frequent skirmishes we had only one more hard fight. I cannot now recall the occasion of this engagement, but it was in the fall of 1864.

Winter Quarters on the Frazier Farm.

We had been quartered for the winter about four miles from Richmond on a Mr. Frazier's farm, the general and staff occupying the lower floor and we couriers the upper story and the cellar. We were called out very suddenly by a demonstration of the enemy on our works on the York River Road and Charles City Road as well as the Nine Mile Road. We had a chain of breastworks thrown up connecting these and other roads, and the enemy were feeling us here. I was ordered by Lieutenant Boyd to go to General Gary and know where he wanted the ordnance train placed. He, as usual, was at the front, and to find him I got into a hot place. The enemy had brought up a large number of pieces of artillery and concentrated their fire upon a certain battery at an angle on our line so as to prevent our infantry from massing at that point to repel their charge upon it when they were ready. We had quite a number there already and when an order was to be carried in or brought out it had to be done at a full run to lessen the risk as to time under fire. At this time the fire was a perfect storm of shot and shell, and it looked as if nothing could escape under it, but my orders were to find General Gary, and all said he was at the battery, and I had to go. I started at a full run to get in the fort, but before I got full under fire met the general and staff coming out at full speed, and the general ordered me to go up our line to the left and put the train on the Nine Mile Road. I started and ran the gauntlet of the infantry fire for a mile. They tried to pick me off, knowing I was carrying orders, but I laid myself on the other side of my horse's neck and body and ran under spur, thus escaping much risk. Just as my course left the line I saw our adjutant, Gen. B. W. Ball, riding a large grey horse just ahead of me, shot down, but found the general was unhurt, but his horse was shot in the stomach. When I got my train properly placed I leisurely returned and on my way back was ordered to take a back road to avoid capture should our line not be held, and when within a mile or so of the fort the enemy made a grand charge, and here, all alone, I had to stop to listen to the grand and awful concert, thanking God that I was spared being there and yet full of awe and tender sympathy for the many poor fellows I knew must be going down. It was the grandest and most sublime experience I ever *heard*, for I could see nothing. The artillery on both sides were in full boom and the fire was so rapid one report could not be distinguished from another except where some piece of large bore belched forth above the din. The war was like a hundred thunder storms combined. Added to this the rifle and musket fire was one continuous rattle or roar, thousands of them on each side, like in conception an immense canebrake afire, only the roar was deafening as well as sickening, and, strange to say, above all this din could be heard the regular huzzahs of the Yankees and the fearful rebel yell in one continuous peel, louder or fainter as success crowned their efforts. The effect on me there by myself in a safe place I can never describe. I now remember I stood listening, thrilled by the magnificence of the sound, at one time elated by its grandeur, and then, as I could hear the exultant yells, I involuntarily pulled off my cap in honor and sympathy for the poor boys I knew must be going to death, and felt I was standing on holy ground and in the presence of the god of battles, and there I alone lifted my voice in prayer to God for mercy to the dying and for our cause. I seemed riveted to the spot, a perfect tumult of feelings rushing over me, as there all by myself I could hear and see, as it were, calmly and weigh matters, as heretofore I had always been in it, and the excitement swept me on, and no time for reflection, I cried aloud, shed tears, and laughed hysterically at the grandness of battle as the different emotions took hold upon me. Those few moments were indelibly impressed on my memory, and I will carry them to my grave, and grand as it was, God grant I may never hear it again.

Pays $2,300 for a Horse.

Duty soon put me in motion again and soon the tumult grew fainter and fainter like a storm spending itself, then a sudden and ominous silence. I pushed on and soon learned the tremendous assault upon our lines had been repulsed with terrific loss to the enemy. This closed all large demonstrations upon our front, and soon all active operations were confined to the south side near Petersburg. We went into winter quarters in the same house above mentioned, and the balance of the winter had a comparatively easy time, outside of the bitter weather and long, cold rides all day and night carrying orders to distant points in all sorts of weather. I remember often coming in late at night during snow and sleet nearly frozen, overcoat frozen so stiff I could hardly get out of it, and when out I would stand it up like a barrel on the end of the long skirt. Here we all took the itch, and constant riding and irritating it made us awfully sore. Often I have come in and on undressing the skin would peel off my legs from seat to ankles in shields and scabs an eighth of an inch thick. We were treated by the surgeon a long time, but with little effect, and I never got over it for two years after the war, if I ever have. Here I broke my horse down, rode and starved him to death, and sent him home by my negro boy who cooked and washed for me. I bought me another, as every man had to furnish his own horse. I gave $2,300 for a very pretty horse, which I kept several years after the war was over. I bought him from Francis Godbold, of Marion, S. C., he getting a furlough to go home to get another one. Here we had vacation from fighting and active dangers and we had many pleasant days and nights together. One of our principal pastimes was to take turn about and run away at night afoot and go to Richmond to the theatre and get back before day before we were missed. We found a tunnel on the York River Railroad entering the city that, strange to say, was unguarded, for every approach to the city was guarded and no one could go in or out without a permit from proper authorities. So our find was a bonanza and hugely we enjoyed it. The plays were fine. I remember seeing Edwin Booth act several times, and saw him the first time he appeared on the stage after his attempt to go over into the Yankee lines to go north, when he was captured and sent back. The theatre was filled that night, as usual, with soldiers, and when Booth came upon the stage they hissed him, yelled, catcalled him, and for an hour made such an uproar that nothing could be done or heard. He begged, explained, laughed, but all to no purpose. The police then tried to put out the discordant element. Then the soldiers put them out and had quite a riot. Finally, after demonstrating their victory and thus showing their disapproval of Booth's course, they allowed him to proceed. He acted that night "Ill Trobadour" and was at his best. I often visited Dr. Baer and Mrs. Baer at Richmond, and they were very kind to me. She was a second mother and I will always cherish her memory. I bought a new black, light felt hat there once and gave $300 for it in Confederate money. Such articles were very scarce.

Often I would have to ride 15 to 20 miles with orders up the line of works and run the gauntlet of all sorts of remarks and ridicule that idle minds could suggest up and down for miles. The soldiers would turn out of their tents or be lolling on the ground in streets and cheer and laugh at these remarks, and it was as much as human nature could endure, though I learned not to get mad and to laugh with them. If one got mad it only made them worse and it would be torture, for he would be handed down the line for miles from mouth to mouth. These soldiers confined here, with no books to read and nothing to do but sleep and eat, became like children and caught on to the least thing to amuse them. It was wonderful to see these lines of breastworks. They ran like a long serpent up and down hill, zigzag and straight as defenses demanded, with a fort built up high every 200 or 300 yards for cannon. and ran this way all around Richmond for miles—perhaps a hundred miles. The breastworks proper between the forts, behind which the infantry camped and fought, were from 4 to 6 feet thick, logs pinned up and filled between with earth, about 6 to 8 feet high. They had a long line of steps like or platform upon which the soldier would step up, fire his rifle and then step down to load while another took his place to fire. The woods were cut down for a thousand yards in front, so an approaching foe found certain death to approach. Just to rear of these lines was a wide street or road for wagons, cavalry or artillery to pass up and down, and then just back of this was miles and miles of a long line of tents, and log huts of every size and description ingenuity could devise for the shelter of the soldiers. It was a perfect curiosity to note the devices and kinds of architecture human ingenuity wrought out for their comfort with the crude means at their hands. Rations at this time were scarce and poor. We generally ate up three days' rations in one, or rather could do it, and often did. Mule meat was common, and on one occasion when my turn came to draw mine, the commissary reached down his hand into the brine in the barrel and handed me a mule's leg with the shoe on it.

Men Become Homesick and Desperate.

Toward the close and about this time our men became gloomy, dispirited; knew we were fighting a forlorn hope, starving almost, getting letters from home that their wives and children were suffering, homesick and desperate were our men. It was proverbial when cheering up and down the line was heard that it was either General Lee or a rabbit. They idolized our immortal Lee and worshipped and trusted him as implicitly as a child would its father. Whenever he appeared on the line every man would turn out on the street bareheaded and wait for him, and such deafening cheering you never heard. A luckless rabbit jumped up would cause the same cheering and a magnetic merriment. You would hear at first a faint and distant murmur like, then a little louder, and louder, then you could just tell it was human voices, then louder and louder it rang, coming like the rush of a coming storm or tornado so fearful was it. On it swelled, gaining in volume and distinctness as it came till it burst upon you in all its fury and swept past. Men like, they were crazed, each one catching the enthusiasm and feeling his duty to aid. Then it swept on and on, growing fainter and fainter as it went till at last it died out as it first came. Men stood and discussed the subject-matter, laughed if it were a rabbit; if it were Lee they did him every homage they could, bowing, throwing their old jackets and caps under his horse's feet, escorting him, stirrup in hand, calling him "Marse Bob", "Uncle Bob", and every conceivable name of endearment. When he had gone out of sight they stood and sat and talked of him, how they loved him and his noble traits. If it was good war news it was discussed, for whatever it was it was passed from mouth to mouth like human telegraphy for miles from one end of the line to the other. It was perfectly wonderful to see it and take it all in. I write these details, as much of it never appears in history and will only be handed down by tradition, and to give posterity some idea of soldiers' life. The vermin in these huts and all on the streets was fearful. Every man was full of body lice; these was no escape. Between them and itch and scratching was the usual luxury.

Toward the close of the winter it became my almost daily duty to carry dispatches from camp to General Ewell's office in Richmond and wait for return ones to camp. In this way I saw much of the city and had rather a good time, saw many officers and generals, and saw a good deal of my friends Dr. and Mrs. Baer, who lived up on Churchill street. The doctor held a high official position in the surgeon general's office, collecting statistics for a surgical work. I saw many pretty girls, and would stop with many at street corners and at gates at the yard and talk to them as if I had known them all my life. They were friendly and patriotic and loved to pet the soldiers, especially if he was a young one. I became reckless, wild and venturesome, and had many escapades with the girls, but with all the temptations never learned to smoke or drink. There were many interesting details and interesting incidents that would take too much time to pen, as this book has already taken a wider scope than at first intended. Many deserters and prisoners fell into our hands, being generally on advanced lines, and they systematically were searched for gold and greenbacks, and it was hid in every conceivable manner—in hat linings, waistbands, lining of coats, boots, between soles of shoes, in bootlegs, and twenty-dollar gold pieces fitted in holes in boot and shoe heels and then leather nailed over them. Our boys always swapped clothes, boots and shoes with them, and it was really amusing to hear the conversations of protest and persuasion used on such occasions, but I must pass on.

Brothers Go Home on Furlough.

Early in February, 1865, I got several letters from home advising of my father's approaching end, as he was old and worn out, and I applied for a furlough to go home twenty days to see him before he died. After the usual red tape was gone through with, as it was my turn and I had never had a leave of absence, I got mine through and started for Richmond in high glee for home, and none but a soldier knows what that meant. I got my government transportation ticket, which I have now in a pocketbook father gave me when I left home and which I carried through the war. It is now in my desk drawer. When I went to Dr. Baer's house who should I meet there but my brother, W. D. Crosland, just from Point Lookout, a Yankee prison. He had been there two years and we had despaired of ever seeing him again, and really thought him dead as we had, for some reason, long since ceased to hear from him. My joy can be imagined.

Poor fellow, he was emaciated, nearly starved to death, sick, lousy, and ragged as a buzzard. I hardly knew him. Poor fellow, how my heart bled for him. He had to remain a day or two to get some new clothes and get in shape to go home and I waited for him, when on the 23rd of February two joyous Confeds started in high glee for home. I was wild with glee and excitement. I recall when we got to Danville I was indignant at the number of worthless citizens around the depot who should have been at the front in the army. I took delight in telling them so, and was further provoked at their sleek, fat pet dogs while we were starving. As the train pulled out I was on the back platform and a terrier jumped on the track. I pulled down on him with a long Colt's revolver and hit him. It infuriated the citizens and greatly shocked my brother, but then I saw no wrong in it. We went on without incident until we ran nearly into Goldsboro, when suddenly our engine was reversed and we backed rapidly for some distance, when we learned that we had been wired that the enemy had got possession of the railroad in our front. The train was put back and carried into Raleigh, N. C. There we spent the night and in the morning learned that there was no railroad communication any further south, that our only chance was to walk home. We immediately made up our minds to set out, which we did, but with much disappointment, as it cut short our time for home and gave us a long, weary and tiresome walk. But we were *going home*, and that compensated for all else. It took us two days to walk to Fayetteville, and near the second night we asked for lodging at a Miss McKethan's, on the north side of the river. It was granted and we found the house kept by two kind old maiden ladies. As soon as they learned our names and that we were Dr. Crosland's sons they could not do enough for us. They put us before a blazing fire and soon the servant handed in a waiter of native wine. It was my first, and as I was weary and foot sore I concluded it would help me, so I drank half a glass, and in ten minutes I was all muddled up. Soon supper was announced, I could hardly get to the table, and when there felt I was acting the fool, but never suspected I was drunk and could not realize what was the matter. I tried to eat, was hungry, but my knife and fork would fall out of my hands. I would be startled at this and seize them up again and try to nerve myself to do better, for I was mortified, but it would happen again. How I got through I cannot tell, but my brother explained, he after-

ward told me, that I never indulged but was overtaken, and they
were sorry for me. He assisted me back to the fire and after a
little the good people, seeing we were worn out, allowed us to
retire. The servant showed us to a beautiful room, a nice bed
with *clean sheets* upon it. I can never forget that, it took us back.
We told the girl to go and tell the ladies to have the sheets taken
off, that we were dirty and every way unfit to occupy their clean
bed, that we would sleep on the floor, but they would not hear to
it and said they would feel offended if we did not use the bed.
Well, we crawled in, a clean bed, a feather bed; it felt so good,
so strange, so like home, after sleeping on hard floors and on the
ground and in the mud so long. We soon fell asleep and knew
nothing till morning, when the servant came and told us it was
time to get up, breakfast was near ready. In a minute she
returned with another waiter of wine. I remembered with shame
the night before, and then thought of the long tramp before us,
and concluded I would take just half the quantity I did at night.
We were soon dressed and were before the fire but a few minutes
before breakfast was announced, and I found myself almost as
drunk as the night before. I here determined never to touch
strong drink again, to which I have adhered all my life. However, I got on tolerably well, and such a breakfast! Well, to a
starving soldier, he alone could appreciate and do justice to it.
These kind ladies would not hear to a cent for lodging, put us up
a large lunch, and we departed with many benedictions upon
them. They directed us to their brother in Fayetteville, who was
a buggy manufacturer. In an hour or two we crossed the river
and found him. He was very kind, but could not find us a horse
and buggy to take us home, but found a little old covered wagon
that was going to Cheraw, and got the man to take us for a consideration. We set out, but the team was poor and weak and we
walked most of the way, riding only in very wet places and when
we gave out. We spent the night at a Mrs. McLochlin's, a kins-
woman of our Uncle Philip Crosland's wife. They treated us
royally and got us off next morning soon with another good lunch.
Without further incident, weary and foot sore, yet all aglow with
excitement and expectation as familiar sights and places came to
our view as we neared home and realized that soon we would be
there, we forgot all and were as if intoxicated and could not con-
tain ourselves. As we came in sight of the old home tears came
to our eyes and on we sped, and about 2 o'clock p. m. we passed

our old private school house and met Throop, the baby, going to school, a very small boy. We and he were crazed with joy and we ran together into the back yard, where the family and house servants were. Our old friends caught on to the news and rushed for us, and such a time we had! On we rushed into the house, Throop ahead telling the news. We rushed into the family bed-room and there found father, mother and younger boys. Well, I can't tell it, only my heart will never forget the time. Father tottering, an old grey-headed invalid, weeping and overjoyed to see his sons—one of whom especially he never hoped to see again. It was a pitiful and tender sight. And mother, mother, who can tell of a mother's love, weeping, laughing, hugging, kissing! Well, it brings my tears even now again as I write it. Father had heart disease and he tried to be calm, but he could not repress himself. Oh, such a time! And when the family were done, in rushed all the old servants—they would have hugged and kissed us, too. Oh, such a time! To think what those two old parents had suffered for us, and now to be reunited! As soon as the excitement had subsided we must then tell it all—how we came! how Brother Willie got out of prison; how we came together; how we got home; and when our tramp was told then a kind, tender mother thought of refreshments, and in they came. We must eat right there, take off our boots and rest, treat our blis-tered feet. Oh, such a father and mother! Well, we spent all the rest of the day right in that sacred room. Father and mother would sit and look at us and weep for joy, and then break off talking again. So we spent two happy days, but more trouble was ahead of us and them.

War Experience Used at Home.

Sherman had been steadily advancing from Columbia on his march northward and Bennettsville lay in his route, and ominous news was reaching our ears continually of his approach and his horrible devastation of property and private rights, and my poor parents saw that soon the accumulation of a life, if not life itself, would pass from them, and now their sons, just home from the enemy, must fly from home before him again. A council was called and it was determined that Brother Willie should take wagons at the largest plantation and haul cotton from the gin house all over the woods where it would not be found and destroyed. I was to do the same at the home place, haul all the bacon into a distant woods, and then take charge of all the slaves, some 30 or 40, and my brother to do the same at the other place, and camp out far from the dwellings in the woods. We supposed the enemy would confine himself to town and beaten roads. This we did. I remained with them and all our horses and mules in a camp one day and night, but we were betrayed by deserting negroes, and the Yankees were upon us before we knew it, though my army training stood me in good hand, for I placed myself on picket duty on the edge of the woods and clearing in a place where I could see any one approaching before they saw me. On Sunday morning I saw a lot of Yankees riding rapidly toward the woods from town. I made all speed back to camp, put horses, mules and negroes all in motion to go deeper into the woods, but soon I saw bluecoats in my front, then to each side, and rear. I saw I had been betrayed and surrounded and gave up for lost, but a faithful boy, Bob Crosland, who had served me and brother in the army, entreated me to run and he would throw them off my track. Appealed to this way I slid off my horse, knowing this my only chance, and ran in the direction I saw clearest of Yankees. I ran some hundred yards and hid in a thick cluster of oak bushes where a pine had blown up by the roots. I heard the Yankees dash up, shooting, and then heard them running in my direction. They came very near me and stopped. They had some of the negroes with them, and I heard them threaten to shoot them if they did not tell where I was. I heard my boy, Olly's Bob we called him, answer at once that "he ran that way," in an opposite direction from one I took. They dashed off that way, but soon returned cursing and swearing they would kill me if found. I felt quite frightened and looked to be found every moment, but a kind Providence protected me. They soon gave up the chase and returned and took the horses and negroes and went back toward town. Still I soon found the woods full of men on foot and horseback. As soon as I dared move I crawled beside a log which a fire had burned hollow. I crawled beside the hollow side and lay close in it. Hardly had I done so before a Yankee stepped over the other end of the log. They were moving about all around me till late in the afternoon, when all became painfully quiet. However, I lay still till night and then knew I could move about safely. I knew all the woods by heart and concluded to make toward the public road on the Marion Road. I moved cautiously along until I came to the edge of the planta-

tion opening near the road. Here I saw the plantation illumin-
ated with thousands of camp fires and the town on fire, and
thousands of moving forms in the distance. I knew this was no
place for me, and started into the woods in another direction
when I ran almost on to a camp fire of a picket post, and the man
on picket duty seeing or hearing me, cried out "Halt." I fell on
my knees and ran as fast as I could grunting like a hog. I heard
the sentinel cursing the damned hog, how he scared him. I knew
then I was safe, but as soon as I felt I was safe I rose and carefully but rapidly plunged into the woods deeper. I determined
to go to the public road near Rev. J. A. W. Thomas's, and carefully approached same. I came out just in front of his house
and cautiously took a survey. I found the rail fence had been
moved across the road and a barricade made against a cavalry
approach. I looked for pickets and found none, but my knowl-
edge of military rules convinced me that I was in between two
posts and I was on unsafe ground. I turned back into the woods,
determined to get clear out of the public highways. Therefore I
struck through the woods, and it was very dark, toward Carter
Branch. I ran into a neighborhood road leading from Marion
Road to Hebron Road, and concluded to go to a little hut near
Pine Plain Church, on Marion Road, and try to get something to
eat, as I had had nothing since breakfast. I got to said hut and
as I stepped in the back door and made myself known to the half-
breeds they were much upset, and said Yankees were coming in
every few moments and for me to get out at once as they would
kill me, and them, too, as they had been hunting me. Said they
would bring me something to eat when things got quiet, and just
as I stepped out of the back door some Yankees walked in the
opposite door. I slipped back some fifty yards in the woods and
laid down in the fence corner and waited for things to get quiet,
but Yankees were coming and going all night and I could hear
them talking and laughing in the house all the time. I concluded,
as it was between midnight and daybreak, it an unsafe place and
took the back track to Carter Branch, on same road, and when I
had got some two miles I took to the swamp at daylight and
finding a long and large poplar log that had fallen with top in
the road. I mounted this log and walked into the swamp until I
came to the other end of it, when I found it hollow, and a very
large one. Into this I crept and lay down and fell asleep, as I
was tired out. I woke up about midday and could see the road

and all passers without being seen. I saw several squads of Yankees passing on horseback, so kept close. Some buzzards saw me, however, and thinking me fit food came and lit on the stump of the tree. I frightened them off, but it made me feel queer. When night came on I ventured out, determined to get some rations at risk of capture, as I was then thirty-six hours without a mouthful. I took up the same road and going some half mile found a log house in the middle of a small field and carefully approached it. I found all safe, went in and found old Aunt Free Sallie David, as she was called by all. I made myself known and what I wanted. She adopted me there and then, told me I need fear nothing, she nor none of her sons would betray me, and to come to her whenever I wanted food; offered to hide me in her house until danger was over, but I was afraid of this as I knew her husband had a bad reputation and never liked father. However, I ate heartily and wrote a note to mother assuring her of my safety and got Sally to put it in her bosom and carry it to mother. Then I returned to my log and spent the remainder of the day. About 10 o'clock at night I came out and went back to Aunt Sally's. She had gotten home, and, what was better, brought a note from mother, who was, of course, overjoyed to know I was safe. Told me when my pursuers came back to town with negroes and my horse they passed the house and held up my overcoat I had left on my saddle in my flight, and told her they had killed me, and she was near crazy. Sallie told me of destruction of all property and that when father had tottered to the gate and begged the Yankees to spare his corn and cotton as it was all he had to feed his children, they cursed him and threatened to throw him in the burning buildings. Sallie gave me all the details of town affairs and doings of the Yankees. Her husband reassured me of my safety and pressed me to stay at night with them, which I consented to do. My confidence in him flattered him and I made a fast friend of him and his grown sons, who were passing to town every day. In the morning, after an early breakfast, I went to my log again, and that day lay there and read Oliver Twist, which my faithful mother sent me to while away the time, and I appreciated little Oliver *asking for more*, for I had had the same fasting experience. About 10 o'clock I was startled by footsteps near me. I listened and I heard some one mount the log I was in. Then I was much concerned. On came the footsteps, seemingly very deliberate, and when on they came till directly over

me my heart was in my mouth. I was sure I had been betrayed
and was captured and perhaps would be shot right there. But I
had little time to think for as I looked up expecting to see my
captors, I saw an old rusty shoe put on the stump and in it was an
old red foot with no sock on it. I knew in an instant that was no
Yankee, and as one foot rested on the stump and the other on the
log the face leaned over and peeped into the log, and I recognized
it on the instant as James Bounds, an old carpenter and screw
builder who had often worked for father. I hardly know who
was frightened the worst, Bounds or myself, as he, on seeing a
man in the log, gave a yell and a bound and went trotting down
the log at a lively rate. I called to him, telling him who I was,
when he came back and sat down and talked an hour with me.
He said some of the Alfred Parish's, a neighbor, had had a lot of
clothing stolen from them and he was on the search for them,
and knowing where this large hollow log was he concluded to look
in it for them, thinking they might have been hid there until
search was over. He said I had frightened him nearly out of his
life, and it was some time before he recovered. I was glad to see
any white face I knew. He left me promising to keep my secret
and I resumed Oliver Twist. That night I went in to Sallie's,
got supper and spent the night, and risked myself next day, as
report was the army was moving on. About 4 o'clock that afternoon as I was sitting talking, Aunt Sallie happened to go to the
door, as she was continually on the watch for me, called out, "Run,
Charlie, run, the Yankees are coming; one is right here." I had
no time to get out, so made for her bed and started under it, when
a voice said, "Come out of that." At once I recognized it as
Brother Willie, and you may be sure I was not only relieved at my
escape, but overjoyed to see him safe and be reunited. He teased
me considerably about running under the bed. Sallie had taken
his new Confederate blue-gray for a blue Yankee uniform. He
recounted his adventures, which were very similar to mine, and
he, too, on escaping from the enemy at the place I now live
(Farmville), where he had congregated negroes and stock from
the plantation his family now owns, had struck out through the
woods and crossed the Marion Road and came to the same hut I
was at, and came near capture, and the occupants, Jacobs, told
him I had been there the night before and gone into the woods in
rear. While there he, too, came near being captured. He then
set out on the same road to find me, and coming to Sallie's house

concluded to go in and enquire if I had been seen, when he saw me getting under the bed in good style.

Well, he was surprised no little when he found how I had fared and had trusted my benefactors, and I could not persuade him it was safe and to join me in resting there. So at his desire we set out and went late that afternoon to the B. F. McGilvery plantation, near by, and got permission to sleep in the ginhouse. We passed a quiet night with sound sleep, and when we woke up the sun was high up, and as we came out our old army servant, Bob, was there calling us. He had come, sent by mother with a note sent to Aunt Sallie for me, to say the army was all gone and it was safe to come home to what was left, and with joy we went. As we came upon the edge of the plantation we began to see the devastation, dead horses, cows, hogs all over the fields, fences all down and burned, roads all blockaded up, and all outhouses burned. First our large ginhouse, with 300 bales of cotton, was gone, then other houses; up town was all chimneys and no houses, and wreck was everywhere. I hardly knew the place. Not a horse or mule remained, all bacon and corn gone, nothing to live upon. Well, when we got to the house we had another joyful reunion and heard with heavy hearts the foul and dastardly treatment our parents had received. Negroes had been made to come in and insult them and help themselves to all clothing in the house or anything else they wished. The dwelling had been set on fire three times, the house robbed of everything and the family had scarce a change of clothing left. Words cannot express the deviltry and destruction inflicted. We went at once to work and went over the fields where the army was camped and collected the fragments of bacon and other meats and corn and other provisions they had lavishly thrown away, and with a few faithful servants who refused to go with the army and loved us, we got enough together to last us a time.

Friends Come to the Rescue.

Soon an incident occurred which I wish my children never to forget. Col. Hamp Rogers, of Brownsville, a big-hearted farmer who lived out of the track of Sherman's march, hearing of our destitution, loaded his wagons with corn, flour, bacon and hams and sent them to us as a present. The proud spirit of my father, heretofore worth near $300,000, was touched and humbled, too, and under other circumstances would have declined to receive the present, but as starvation was staring his family in the face he accepted the donation with many thanks, with the understanding he be allowed to pay for it when able. Ill health and hard work had already nearly done up my father, but the late and terrible reverses and intense excitement was too much for him, and he took to bed and sank rapidly worse, and amid a weeping family went to his Master on the 29th of March, 1865.

We foresaw the end was near, and though my furlough was out and my brother was to report back to the army, we determined to see the end and try and leave the family as well provided for as possible. We laid the remains of our father to rest at his birth-place, the old Philip Crosland place, and have since moved them to Oak Ridge Cemetery, Bennettsville. Our robbery was so complete that we were compelled to dress the body in an old darned, castaway suit of clothes, and in a common pine coffin stained with soot and turpentine. It hurt us much, but was the best we could do. In a few days we made up our minds that we must return to our commands, and tearfully we set out after a sad parting from our widowed mother, with her strong arm she had leaned on so long gone. Here let me say, just before our departure Henry Rogers and Col. Ham. Rogers again sent their loaded wagons to the door of our widowed mother begging to help her while her boys went to fight their battles. God bless their memory. He will reward them.

Proud Possessors of Mules.

We took our two army negro boys and started our tramp to Richmond, as there was no railroad in operation but near General Lee's army. The first day we marched to Cheraw and spent the night some five miles the other side at a Mr. Barrentine's. Next day we reached Wadesboro, our heels blistered, and were cared for by a Mrs. Lisles. The next day we struck out for Albermarle Courthouse, as we heard that it was probable if we could reach Salisbury we might strike railroad connection to Richmond. We made this detour westward to avoid Sherman's advancing army northward, not knowing where he would strike for. Just before we reached Albermarle we met several squads of Confederate soldiers coming home, who all told us the war was over and General Lee had surrendered. We did not believe them and concluded they were deserters. What, General Lee surrender! We regarded that an impossibility, absurd, it had never dawned on us such a thing could be possible, such an exalted admiration and faith had we for and in him. We scouted the idea. On we went, arrived near night, worn out, at Albermarle, but heard the same story from all sources. We lodged at an hotel here, paying in Confederate money, which still passed though almost worthless, rested our weary limbs, and awoke next morning with hope of better news, but concluding to rest here a day before going further and see if reports could be true. Soon General Gardener, a quartermaster general stationed here pressing horses for army and gathering supplies, advised us to go home, that our cause was lost. Still we doubted, and soon a colonel of infantry came in with his stars on his collar; then a general, who told us it was true, Lee had surrenderd and they were from his army and had witnessed the surrender. Well, I can never make my feelings understood but to a loyal fellow soldier of Lee's army. When the news dawned on my understanding as a fact, I stood in the road and cried like a child, like my heart would break, saying Lee has surrendered after all his gallant fight, remembering all we had gone through with him, then when I remembered that the cruel war was over and that we were free to go home to the family and remain, no more starving, freezing, fatigue and danger of death and capture, I laughed aloud. Then remembering past glory of Lee was gone, what surrender involved, I was ashamed of my mirth and cried again. For several hours we both talked over the fact, and laughed and cried alternately like two hysterical women. Home now was our next thought, and afterward what? No horse or mule there to plow for a living, it was a gloomy prospect. There was a large drove of mules and horses the above quartermaster general had pressed in for the government in a lot in the town. We went to the general and tried to describe our condition at home after Sherman's march, and asked him to let us have four mules, one each for ourselves and boys. He hesitated a while and then told us to go and pick them out, taking our receipt for them in case he should ever have to account for them. We could find no bridles, so I went to the wagon yard of the quartermaster and gave a driver (negro) $100 for a plow line off a covered wagon. We took this and cut in four pieces and tied each piece around the lower jaw of the mules we had selected, and mounted bareback, the other end of the line just long enough for us to reach it. We set out this way for home, down that long, steep series of hills, as proud of our luck as kings. The country was infested with robbers and deserters, and we feared violence all the way, for it was a wild country. We rode steadily, however, without any rest or molestation, fearing any ill luck, till we reached Mr. Barrentine's, near Cheraw, who had kindly entertained us on our way up. He received us again kindly and rejoiced with us over our good luck. We spent the night with him and next day, Sunday morning, the 16th day of April, set out for home and soon were on Marlboro soil again to stay. The sight of mules agitated many on the road and all wanted to stop and talk and buy us out, but we had no time to idle and pushed on, and well do I remember as we crossed the creek bridges and rose the hill and came upon the main street church services were over and the sidewalk was full of people, men, ladies and children coming home from service, and a pretty swell we cut leaning forward to grip our line, our pants up to our knees, bareback and sore and skinned from said fact. We made a triumphant entry into the town. We were at once the center of attraction as all knew as at once, and four mules cut a sensation. We brought first news of Lee's surrender, as we had no mails or wires running since Sherman's destructive march. All were pained at the news and very sad. Several old gentlemen jumped off the pavement and came, Sunday as it was, offering to buy our mules. We were offered $300 apiece for them in gold, but they represented meat and bread for our family and a starting of shattered fortunes which was more than gold, so to all we said no. When we rode into the back yard at home there was joy again on our good mother's face to see her two boys again at home, and to see the mules which meant so much to us.

We were never called upon to return these mules and they were the means of a new start in life, and here must end these reminiscences of my war experiences as peace had dawned upon all the land.

CHAS. CROSLAND.

I omitted to say Gary's Brigade was composed of The Hampton Legion, the Seventh South Carolina Cavalry, the Eighth Georgia Cavalry Regiment, and the Twenty-fourth Virginia Cavalry Regiment. The cronological order of the different battles I cannot vouch for, nor the dates, as time has dimmed my memory and I had no means of keeping up dates. Kept no diary and trusted alone to memory.   C. C.

Made in United States
Orlando, FL
22 March 2026

79568422R00053